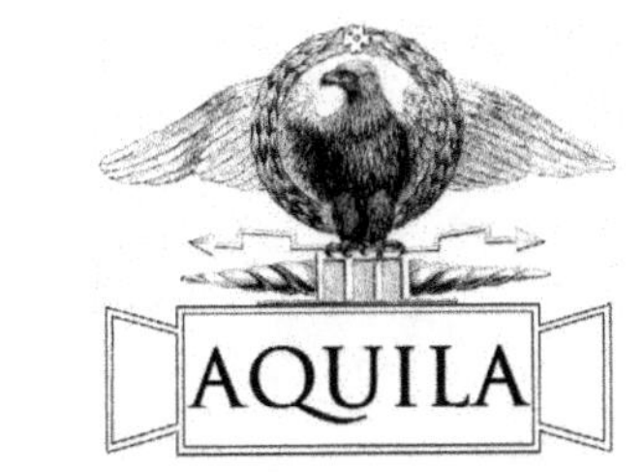

HARRISBURG, ARKANSAS

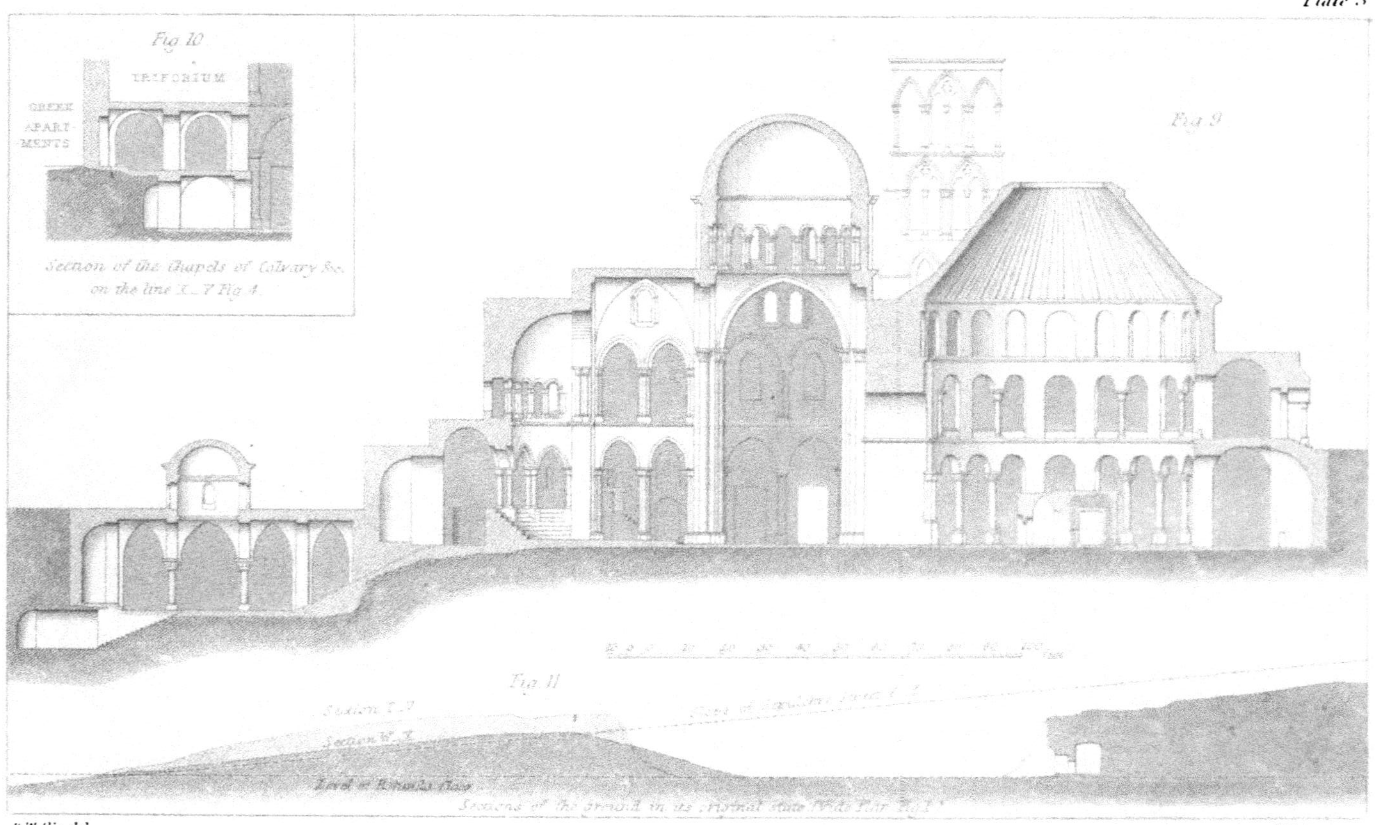

R. Willis del.

LONGITUDINAL SECTION OF THE CHURCH OF THE HOLY SEPULCHRE.

THE
ARCHITECTURAL HISTORY
OF THE
Church of the Holy Sepulchre
AT
JERUSALEM.

BY THE REV. ROBERT WILLIS, M.A., F.R.S.

JACKSONIAN PROFESSOR OF THE UNIVERSITY OF CAMBRIDGE.

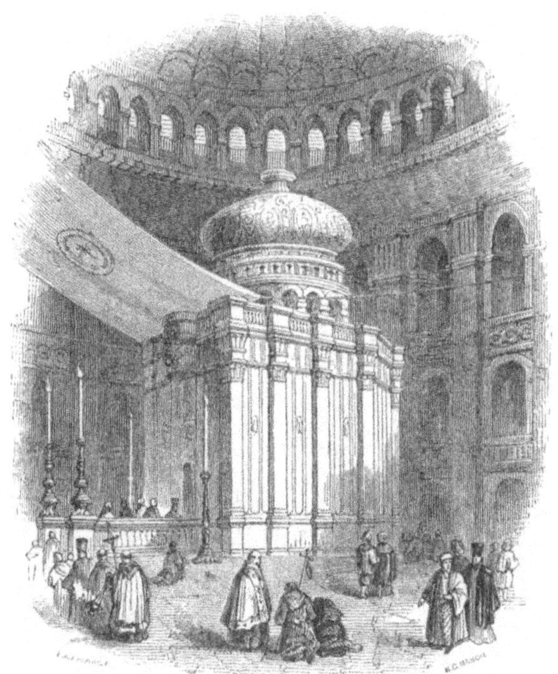

The Holy Sepulchre in its present state. (See page 34.)

LONDON:
JOHN W. PARKER, WEST STRAND.
CAMBRIDGE: JOHN DEIGHTON.

M.DCCC.XLIX.

TABLE OF CONTENTS.

SUPPLEMENTARY NOTES.

LIST OF ENGRAVINGS.

N. B.—The present Work is inserted entire in the Second Edition of the HOLY CITY, of which it forms Chapter III., Vol. II., and which is published simultaneously with it.

ADDENDA ET CORRIGENDA.

Page	Line		Error.	Correction.
10	note [1] 8		Appendix (A.)	Note C, p. 157.
27	text 5	from top	(fig. 1.)	(fig. 12.)
28	— 17	- -	arch A	arch H.
30	— 3	from bottom	South	East.
—	— 2	- - -	North	South.
—	— 1	- - -	East	North.
31	— 10	from top	northern	western.
38	note [2],	last line of,	*after* below.	*insert* p. 58.
66	note [2],	last line of,	*insert*, vide Holy City Vol. I. Supp. p. 60, where it appears that Felix Fabri in 1480 (namely 70 years before Bonifacius) likewise selected one of this group of tombs, as resembling the Holy Sepulchre.	
68	note	5 from bottom, in second col.	*after* Temple,	*insert* vide H.C. Vol. II. p. 341. and Vol. I. Supp. p. 95.
83	note [6]	last line of,	Vide Appendix	Vide Note C. p. 157.
94	text 5	from top	North	South.
95	— 5	- -	*after* altar	*insert* (33.)
98	note [1]	This note is more fully elucidated at p. 164, under the description of Fig. 5.		
108	Sect. IX.	Compare the Plan, Fig. 1, with the corresponding sections in Fig. 11. Plate III.		
122	text 14	from top	(H L Fig. 1)	(H I Fig. 1 and Y Fig. 3.

THE

ARCHITECTURAL HISTORY

OF

The Holy Sepulchre.

I.

INTRODUCTORY REMARKS.

THE Church or group of Churches which is the subject of the following pages, was in its original form erected by the Emperor Constantine for the pious purpose of protecting and venerating that Sepulchral cavern which was believed to have been the very Tomb in which the Body of our Lord was laid. The buildings received, in accordance with the custom of that period, the name of the Martyrium of the Resurrection. They have long since disappeared, and others have been in turn erected and destroyed on the same site, until at length they have been brought to the state in which they now are. But during all ages of Christianity, and under all their vicissitudes, these structures have remained the great centre of pilgrimage; to obtain this site, the best blood and wealth of Europe was poured forth in the Crusades, and before and after that hopeless struggle to retain Christian possession of it, no difficulties, dangers, or insults, were powerful enough to deter the crowds of pilgrims who annually went forth to visit the scenes of their Saviour's sufferings and triumphant Resurrection. Whether or no these sacred events took place upon the spots that were so confidently assigned as their true localities, has been of late years very warmly contested. But this is not essential to the question. Those who erected the buildings, and those who visited them, were alike convinced of the genuineness of the traditions; and therefore the influence of these buildings upon Ecclesiastical Architecture is wholly irrespective of the enquiry into the true localities. And it is as a branch of the history of Ecclesiastical Architecture alone that I purpose to treat the subject at present.

But, considering the vast influence that was exercised during the middle ages by the veneration for sacred localities of all kinds, as well as for relics, and the numerous Churches which were erected solely for the purpose of affording objects of pilgrimage, by distinguishing such sacred localities and making them as it were a mark for pilgrims; it is evident that the buildings upon that spot which was of all others the most sacred, must be of exceeding interest in teaching us the principles upon which such Martyria were arranged.

In saying this, I by no means intend to throw doubts upon the truth of that tradition which has fixed the site of the Holy Sepulchre within the Church in question; for I am myself fully convinced of the genuineness of that site. But that question has been treated by much abler hands than mine, and requires an investigation of the entire topography of the City, which I am not qualified to undertake, if even it were included in the Architectural question, which it is not, as I have endeavoured to shew[1].

[1] Since these pages were written, an attempt has been made by Mr Fergusson, in his Essay on the Topography of Jerusalem, to shew that not only the present site is not genuine, but that the Martyrium of Constantine was erected

It is very curious and interesting, but at the same time most melancholy, to trace the process by which the cravings of the simpleminded and ignorant crowd of pilgrims to behold and to touch every spot where some event of the sacred narrative took place, led to a gradual accumulation of local appropriation, which has ended in a confident indication not only of every place where every historical event happened, but also of places connected with the parables, which we have no reason to believe were other than fables invented for our edification. A visit to the "House of the Rich Man," or a sight of the "Stone which the builders rejected," are very apt to excite the wrath and disgust of our better informed but somewhat hasty modern travellers, and lead them to denounce the Monks and Pilgrims of the middle ages as a pack of knaves or credulous fools, and the entire body of local tradition as a system of premeditated imposture, no one portion of which deserves the least credit.

This is an error in the opposite extreme, by which much valuable truth is rejected. It is, unfortunately, impossible to deny the credulity, or even the imposture in many cases; neither can we wonder at the disgust and indignation which must arise in the mind of every sincere and right-thinking person at the sight of such a

in another part of the city, and is no other than the present Mosque of Omar. But this theory is, in my opinion, perfectly untenable, although, if it were true, it would not very seriously interfere with the following dissertation. However, leaving the topographical part of the controversy in the hands of my friend the author of the Holy City, I shall make a note of Mr Fergusson's statements as I proceed, and now shall merely express my regret that he should have permitted himself to fling abuse and contempt so unsparingly upon preceding authors. His hypothesis is certainly quite new, and nobody is likely to dispute the credit of it with him.

mass of absurdity and falsehood, and of mean and low passions and feelings, fostered into full activity in a land and in a city that ought to excite far different and holier feelings. But however difficult it may be to separate the after-growth of credulity from the true original tradition around which it has accumulated, it must be remembered that it may have preserved to us the memory of the spot where some great and leading event took place; and, for example, I am not prepared to reject the traditional site of the Sepulchre, because I find close to it an altar absurdly pretending to mark the very place where the soldiers divided the vestments.

With respect to the Church which is the immediate object of this Essay, Robinson has well and calmly stated the difficulties that at first sight present themselves to the mind of a traveller. "The place of our Lord's Crucifixion, as we are expressly informed, was without the gate of the ancient city, and yet nigh to the city[1]. The Sepulchre, we are likewise told, was nigh at hand, in a garden, in the place where Jesus was crucified[2]. It is not, therefore, without some feeling of wonder that a stranger unacquainted with the circumstances, on arriving in Jerusalem at the present day, is pointed to the place of Crucifixion and the Sepulchre in the midst of a modern city, and both beneath the same roof. This latter fact, however unexpected, might occasion less surprise; for the Sepulchre was nigh to Calvary. But beneath the same roof are further shewn...various other places said to have been connected with the history of the Crucifixion, most of which it must have

[1] Heb. xiii. 12; John xix. 20. The same is also implied in John xix. 17; Matt xxvii. 32.

[2] John xix. 41, 42.

been difficult to identify, even after the lapse of only three centuries; and particularly so at the present day, after the desolation and numerous changes which the whole place has undergone[3]."

The difficulty thus laid down with respect to the locality, is fully discussed in "the Holy City." The places, which are to this day so confidently and credulously pointed out within this Church, may be enumerated as follows: (1) the Holy Sepulchre. (2) The hole in the Rock in which the Cross was fixed. (3) The holes on each side in which the thieves' crosses were fixed. (4) The spot upon which the Crucifixion or actual nailing to the Cross took place, which the Latins assert to have been done previously to the elevation of the Cross. (5) The stone upon which the Body was laid after it was taken down from the Cross, and where it was wrapped in linen with spices. (6) The place where the soldiers divided the vestments. (7) The spot where the friends of our Lord stood afar off during the Crucifixion. (8) Where the women stood during the anointing of the Body, &c. (9) Where the women stood over against the Sepulchre. (10) Where our Lord appeared to Mary Magdalene as a gardener. (11) Where He appeared to the Virgin Mary. (12) The Prison in which He was detained while the preparations were making for the Crucifixion. (13) The place where the Crosses were discovered by Helena. (14) The place where she sat while the digging was proceeding for that purpose. Beside these places, which are distinguished by altars and especial chapels, or else by stones let into the pavement, there are some relics removed from other places,

---

[3] Bib. Res. Vol. II. p. 64.

such as the column of Flagellation, of Mocking, &c. Some of the places above enumerated have no connexion with the Scripture narration, but belong to legendary addition, as Nos. 11 and 12. But it will appear in the course of the following history, that with the exception of (1) The Sepulchre, (2) the hole for the Cross, and (13) the place where the Crosses were found, not one of the above sacred localities or *stations* are mentioned by any writer previous to the conquest of Jerusalem by the Crusaders, at the end of the eleventh century, and the hole for the Cross appears for the first time in the narration of Arculfus in the ninth century; for before this time we only hear of Golgotha (or Calvary) in general terms, which, as Robinson has observed, is scripturally connected with the site of the Sepulchre. The place where the Crosses were found belongs to the legend of their discovery, and thus, after all, with this exception, the original tradition of the Sepulchre stands alone and separated by many centuries from the heap of credulous rubbish which has so disgusted and repelled modern travellers and writers, and which has mainly induced them to seek arguments for the rejection of the Sepulchre itself. Many of the holy places or stations probably arose from the mediæval practice of dramatising the sacred narratives, or presenting them in the most palpable forms of representation to the senses of the ignorant crowd. We may therefore regard such stations as having been at first established as memorials, or altars, for the purpose of fixing the succession of leading events more certainly in the memory, and that in time they came, by an easy transition, to be considered as having been placed upon the very spots upon which each event happened.

I will now proceed to the Architectural History of the Church, the investigation of which has formed the subject of Lectures that I have delivered at Cambridge and at the Royal Institution in London, at various times, but has been considerably matured by the information which these Lectures have procured for me from the kindness of many of my friends; and, amongst others, from the excellent author of the "Holy City," whose knowledge of the locality, and extensive researches into the literature of the subject, has been of great service to me. I have gladly, therefore, availed myself of his kind request that I would append these pages to his valuable history.

II.

CHURCH OF THE SEPULCHRE IN GENERAL.

The buildings on this site have been repeatedly ruined and rebuilt, and otherwise altered from time to time; but the principal changes which we shall have to consider may be briefly recapitulated as follows[1].

The first edifices that were erected to do honour to this place were those of Constantine, which were dedicated in the year 335. These were ruined in the Persian invasion of Chosroes, in 614, and restored by Modestus fifteen years afterwards. Jerusalem was taken by the Mahometans in 637; but the sacred buildings in question were not injured by them at that time. In 1010, they were, however, utterly and purposely de-

[1] The History of the Holy City, to which I beg to refer my readers, contains a detailed account of these events in the order of their occurrence, but of course mixed up with the general narrative. My object in the following Essay requires that I should separate the history of this church entirely from the history of Jerusalem.

stroyed by the order of the Kalif Hakem. Thirty years afterwards, permission was obtained by the Emperor Constantine Monomachus to rebuild them, which was effected under the Patriarch Nicephorus, about fifty years before the entry of the Crusaders.

They, during their reign in Jerusalem, greatly increased the buildings; and, after their expulsion, no important changes took place until the unhappy fire, which, in 1808, so greatly damaged the Church, as to necessitate the entire reconstruction of its central portions. All these successive changes I shall proceed to examine at length.

Each successive restoration of these buildings introduced changes of form and style, in accordance with the methods of building that happened to prevail at the moment; and we have, therefore, according to the statement just made, five distinct periods of the building to examine, namely, (1) the buildings of Constantine; (2) those of Modestus; (3) those of Monomachus; (4) those of the Crusaders; and, finally, (5) those that at present exist.

Now, although the historians relate that in the Persian invasion, and at the demolition by the Mahometans in 1010, the buildings upon this site were, as it were, uprooted from the earth; it must be remembered that the destruction of a complex mass of building, like that in question, is by no means so easy: nor is it ever effected by a hostile force, so as to obliterate the foundations, for the ruins of the vaults and walls necessarily protect the lower part of the buildings. When a building is taken down by friendly hands, the materials are carefully removed as fast as they accumulate. But this systematic process is not likely to be carried on by men working under the influence of malicious violence, whose sole purpose is to disfigure, and render untenable, the object of their fury. They are satisfied when the perfect structure is converted into a misshapen heap of ruins. But those who, when the storm has passed, return with friendly hands to clear away the rubbish, and rebuild the fallen walls, are sure to find the original foundations, much of the lower part of the walls, and many of the vaults, still entire. The original plan of the buildings, therefore, can never be lost, under such circumstances; but it may be departed from during the rebuilding, for two opposite reasons. In the first place, the funds may not be sufficient to reconstruct the whole of the buildings, or even to construct the part of them which has been selected, on so magnificent a scale as before. Or, on the other hand, the funds may be so large as to tempt an increase of magnitude and grandeur. It is true, however, that buildings founded, as these are, upon a rock, require so little depth of foundation-building, that they are more easily eradicated, and afford less temptation for the employment of old foundations in rebuilding, than structures which are erected upon ground that requires deep trenches to be made, and massive subwalls to afford a footing for the superstructure. Such substructures necessarily escape a hostile destruction. In our present building, the original levelling and cutting down of the rock will be found to afford the best traces of the former dispositions. But all these causes have influenced, from time to time, the remarkable group of buildings which I propose to examine. The authorities from which our knowledge of the arrangements of the buildings are derived, are the numerous pilgrimages and chronicles of the middle ages; and, by comparing and collating these, and by a constant reference to the site, I hope to be able to shew, that a tolerably consistent architectural history of these vicissitudes of plan may be drawn out.

As the Churches in question form an exceedingly complex group, and we are necessarily better acquainted with the more recent structures, than with the older ones, we must take the history in a reverse order, and begin with the fourth period, namely, by describing the whole as it stood from the time of the Crusaders, until the fire of 1808[1], which however has not affected the plan of the buildings.

The Church, in its general plan, may be described as a Romanesque cruciform structure, having a circular nave to the West, a North and South transept, and a short Eastern limb or choir terminated by an apse. An aisle runs round the circular nave, on three of its sides. Also there is an aisle at the end of each transept, and on the East and West sides of each transept; and an aisle passes round the apse, and has chapels radiating from it, in the usual manner. Projecting from the East end, but lying to the South of the central line of the edifice, is a chapel, termed the chapel of S. Helena. The Eastern aisle of the South transept is occupied by chapels in two floors, the upper floor having the chapel of the Crucifixion. The principal, and at present the only, entrance to the Church, is at the South front of this Southern transept. Moreover, the triforium of the

---

[1] Plate 2 is a Plan, and Plate 3 a longitudinal section of the Church and its chapels as they appeared during the fourth period; this plan is based upon a most elaborate survey, for which I am indebted to the kindness of my excellent friend J. Scoles, Esq., who laid it down in the year 1825. In Appendix (A) I have explained my authorities for the sections at length.

Church is an entire floor, extending over the whole of the side-aisles, and was, on its first completion, accessible from one end to the other, and, indeed, all round the Church; but was subsequently obstructed by party walls, erected for the accommodation of some of the various sects who have divided the Church amongst them.

The circular nave or Rotunda was wholly erected with circular arches, but the Eastern part of the Church with pointed arches; having, however, round arches in the windows, according to the usual practice at the early period of the pointed style. In the centre of the Rotunda is placed the principal object, for the protection and veneration of which the entire structure was planned; and before I proceed to the detailed description of that structure, I must investigate the arrangement and history of the Sepulchral Cavern, which had so vast an influence upon it.

III.

ON THE HOLY SEPULCHRE, AND ROCK-TOMBS IN GENERAL.

In the centre of the Rotunda, as I have already said, there stands a small Chapel or *edicula*, twenty-six feet in length, and eighteen in breadth, having its interior divided into two small apartments, the inner one of which is said to be the actual Sepulchral Chamber "hewn out of a rock," in which the body of our Lord was deposited. Its present appearance, which is, at first sight, that of an artificial construction of masonry, is explained by saying that the architects of Constantine levelled the ground all round the Cave, leaving that portion of rock, within which the chamber had been excavated, to stand up as an isolated block, and that the exterior and interior of this block has been cased with ornamental architecture, so as to give it its present artificial appearance.

To enable my readers to judge of the probability of this account, I must digress into a short examination of the arrangement and form of the Jewish and Roman Sepulchres; for it must be remembered, that the Sepulchre in question, originally formed for a wealthy Jew, "his own new tomb," "wherein never man before was laid," was altered into its present condition by a Roman emperor, more than three centuries afterwards.

Every traveller bears witness to the innumerable rock-sepulchres which exist in the valleys round about Jerusalem. The general mode of construction is, in the words of Robinson, that "a door in the perpendicular face of the Rock, usually small and without ornament, leads to one or more small chambers excavated from the rock, and commonly upon the same level with the door. Very rarely are the chambers lower than the door, the walls in general are plainly hewn; and there are occasionally, though not always, niches or resting-places for the dead bodies. To obtain a perpendicular face for the door, advantage was sometimes taken of a former quarry; or an angle was cut in the rock with a tomb in each face; or a square niche or area was hewn out in a ledge, and then tombs excavated in all three of its sides. All these expedients are seen particularly in the northern part of the valley of Jehoshaphat, and near the Tombs of the Judges. Many of the doors and fronts of the tombs along this valley are now broken away, leaving the whole of the interior exposed[1]."

But the interior arrangements are minutely described by the accurate Schultz, as follows. "Amongst the Sepulchres of Jerusalem we find two modes of arrangement, which, however, resemble each other in one respect, that they are both divided into two parts. A low door gives admission to a small vestibule, within which a similar door, opposite to the first, leads to the sepulchral chamber. Thus far the two kinds are alike; but their difference is that in one, the niches (or *loculi*[2]) are cut out of the rock with their longest dimension *perpendicular* to the sides of the apartment, as in the plan fig. A. Thus a moderately sized chamber is sufficient to afford room for ten or twelve bodies.

Fig. A.

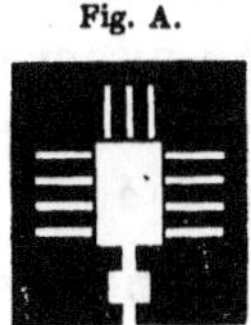

Fig. B.

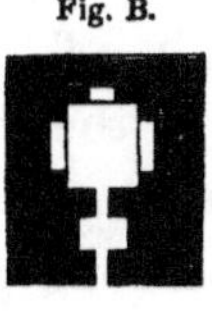

In the second, narrower niches (or *loculi*) are hewn out of the two sides of the cavern, on either side one, having the long dimension *parallel* to the side of the apartment, (as in fig. B.), and in these either the body was laid or a sarcophagus placed. The side of the room opposite to the door has very frequently a little niche that would receive the body of a child, and often a place for a lamp. This latter mode of arrangement,

[1] Robinson, Bib. Res. Vol. I. p. 522.

[2] I employ this word *loculus* as a convenient general term for the receptacle of the body in a sepulchral structure, whether that receptacle be a grave, a chest, a cavity in the rock, or any other of the forms that are to be found.

which occurs amongst others in the Tombs of the Kings, was, in my opinion, reserved for the sepulchres of rich and distinguished persons[1]."

It appears, from this description, that the dead were always deposited in a cavity hewn out of the sides of the chamber, but that in one case they were laid at right angles to the side of the room in a long *deep loculus*, and in the other case, parallel to the side of the room in a *shallow loculus*.

These two classes of receptacles are to be found in the rock-sepulchres of other nations. The first kind, however, is by no means so common as the second. The Egyptians appear to have occasionally employed such cavities for the deposit of their mummies, and they occur in the tombs of Petra. Later, in the Christian catacombs of Rome, the discovery of a few loculi of this form in the cemetery of St Ciriaca, is mentioned as a most unusual arrangement[2].

But the second position of the body, which is by far the most usual amongst all the nations of antiquity who employed the sepulchral chamber, is the one which interests us the most, as it was undoubtedly the form of the so-called Holy Sepulchre[3].

It is scarcely necessary for me to remind my readers that the Jews simply laid their dead in the tomb, swathed up in linen, with aromatics, but without employing either the elaborate embalmment of the Egyptians, or their complex coffins. Those Romans who did

---

[1] Schultz, Jerusalem, p. 97.

[2] Monumenti primitivi delle Arti Christiani, Rome, 1844, pp. 110, 225.

[3] Throughout this dissertation I employ the term "Holy Sepulchre" to designate that which is exhibited under that title in the church in question, without necessarily assuming it to be the genuine sepulchre of the gospels.

not burn the corpse, deposited it in a coffin, or stone sarcophagus, which was closed with a lid; and this was the practice of the Greeks. But it is also known that the early Greeks, Etrurians, and other nations, deposited their dead, dressed in the armour or robes of state which they wore when living, and simply laid them thus upon a stone or bronze couch, protecting them, like the Jews, from spoliation or from wild beasts only by securing, and sometimes concealing, the doors of the sepulchral chambers.

It is evident that the form and arrangement of these sepulchral chambers must have been designed with especial reference to the manner in which the bodies of their future tenants were intended to be deposited within them. In many instances the sarcophagus, couch, or other resting-place, is hewn out of the solid rock, and thus must have been left standing out from the floor, or projecting from the sides, when this apartment was first excavated. When the stone couch was employed, its surface was either level, or merely hollowed out an inch or two in depth, to afford a resting-place; and a raised part is often left at the head, to serve as a pillow, or a round cavity cut for the same purpose. Such couches are found in the Etruscan rock-tombs, and in those of Greece and Asia Minor. I am not now speaking of the stone benches in such tombs, which served as resting-places, or shelves, for the cinerary urns, &c. In the Jewish tombs of Syria, however, the recess in the side of the chambers appears to have been always employed. But even this admits of great variety[4]. In

[4] Many of the rock sepulchres around Jerusalem belonged to Romans or Greeks, Pagan or Christian, the inhabitants of the city after its occupation by the Romans, and it is exceedingly difficult to distinguish the

its simplest form, it is a rectangular opening or cavity in the face of the rocky side of the tomb, the bottom of it being usually higher than the floor of the chamber; and its length and depth just sufficient to admit of a human body being deposited in it. Often its upper surface or soffit is curved into an arch, which is either segmental or semicircular; and this, too, is its usual form when a sarcophagus is deposited in it.

Loculi [1] of this description are sometimes cut in the sides of the chamber, one above the other, in two or more tiers.

Lastly, the bottom of the cavity is often excavated so as to form a sarcophagus, or stone-coffin, so deep as to allow a horizontal stone to be placed upon its edges; thus the arrangement practically resembles a sarcophagus placed in an arched recess sufficiently deep to enclose it completely.

As a Syrian example of this latter form, I may quote certain rock tombs that exist near Khan Kesrawan, between Sidon and Tyre; for the drawings of one of which I am indebted to Mr Scoles.

Fig. X is a plan of this tomb, and fig. Y a section. As in Dr Schultz's description, we have first a low door-way, two feet nine inches square, which was formerly closed by a stone-door, the sockets for whose

genuine Jewish sepulchre from the latter. But to this latter class appear to belong the catacombs on the Hill of Offence south of Jerusalem, which are said to resemble the tombs of Asia Minor, and some of which have Greek inscriptions. Also some at least of the architecturally decorated catacombs and tombs, of which more below.

[1] The only example of sarcophagi at Jerusalem is in the so-called "Tomb of the Kings," wherein they were placed in semicircularly arched recesses in the sides of the apartment. The general rule of the Jews appears not to have been to employ coffins of any kind.

pivots still remain (K). The form of this is a perfectly simple and unornamented square, as shewn in elevation

Fig. X.

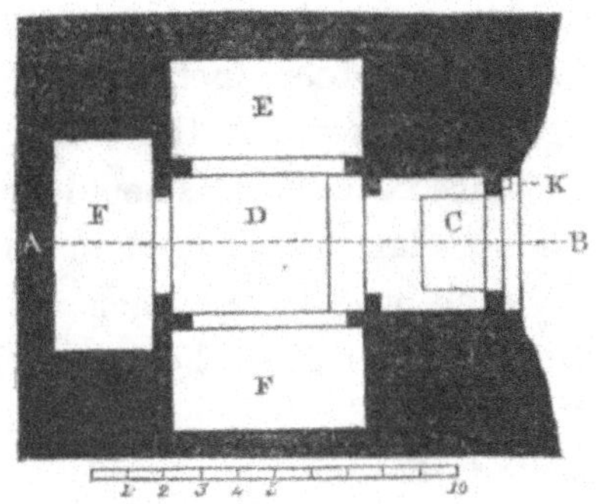

Fig. Y.

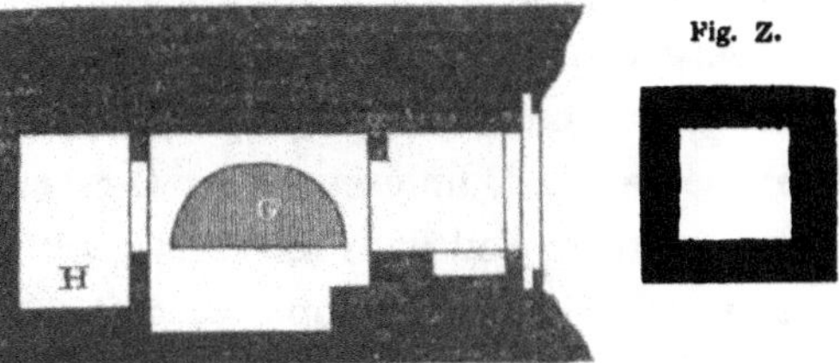

Fig. Z.

in fig. Z. This admits to a little vestibule, C, the floor of which is sunk, probably to receive moisture; and from which a second entrance, opposite to, and rather lower than, the first, admits to the sepulchral chamber D, the dimensions of which are but five feet three inches in length, and about four in width. It is only four feet nine high, and is flat-ceiled. Each of three sides, however, has a sepulchral loculus, E, F, F, for the reception of a body. As the three are alike in form, the elevation of one of them, G, in fig. Y, corresponds to the section of the other, H, in the same figure.

An arch, G, pierced in the side of the chamber, is the opening to the loculus; and the lower margin of this arch is two feet above the floor of the chamber. But at the bottom of this arch a sunk receptacle (as at H) is formed, eighteen inches in depth, to receive the body, as shewn by the section; and herein lies the principal difference between this sepulchral chamber and Schultz's second class of Jerusalem tombs. (Fig. B, above). They each have their antechamber and recessed loculi; but in the latter class there is no hollow or chest sunk in the bottom of the arch, so that the body was simply deposited thereon.

In the present example, as no ledge appears at the back or sides of the loculus to afford a resting-place for a horizontal slab to cover the bodies, it may be inferred that they were left uncovered; and that the stone-door of the outer chamber was the only means by which the sepulchre was secured, unless indeed the vertical arches of the loculi were closed with masonry.

The arch of the loculus opposite to the door is narrower than the others, on account of the dimensions of the apartment. But as the cavity expands behind the opening, it is still long enough to receive the corpse of a full-grown man, but not if enclosed in a coffin.

This form of a loculus occurs in various other districts. Texier[1] has given drawings of a rock-chamber at Nacoleia, in Asia Minor, the general arrangement of which is similar to this, but it has no vestibule, and the rude ornament of the doorway shews it to belong to a very early period; while another sepulchre at the same place, with a similar doorway, has stone couches

[1] Texier, Déscription de l'Asie Mineur, Pl. 57.

against the walls in lieu of these arched recesses and square chests of stone. He has also given engravings of another sepulchral excavation at Nacoleia, with these arched recesses, the front of which has a deep portico with rude columns.

At Urgur[2] a chamber occurs which has on each of three sides an oblong rectangular opening, about eighteen inches from the floor, instead of an arch. The one opposite to the door is provided with a deeply sunk cavity, like those under the arches of fig. Y, above. But the lateral openings have only a shallow sinking at the bottom of their recesses. A rude early portico and atrium, of slightly Egyptian character, is in front of this cavern.

The arched recess, with the hollow chest or stone coffin below, (as in figs. X, Y, Z) abounds in the Christian catacombs both of Rome and of Naples, where it appears to have been reserved for the richer or more distinguished persons. The fortunate discovery of an inscription attached to one of these[3], in which the monument itself is mentioned, has taught us that its proper name was ARCOSOLIUM. In these, however, the cavity is covered by an horizontal slab, which is supported by a narrow ledge at the back and sides, and rests in front upon the front wall of the *loculus*[4].

---

[2] Texier, Pls. 92, 93.

[3] The inscription is preserved in the pallazzo Rondanini at Rome (Mon. Prim. d. Arti Christiani, p. 85.) The pagans employed the word *solium* for the *arca*, or sarcophagus, in which they enclosed the dead body, and the Christians applied the same term to the chest in which relics of their martyrs were kept under an altar. (Ib. p. 96.) *Solium* is also a *bath*, which a sarcophagus resembles. The compound word *Arcosolium* very fitly represents the peculiar form of sepulchral monuments to which it was applied.

[4] Mr Wilde, in his Narrative of a Voyage to Madeira, &c. (Dublin, 1840, Vol. II. p. 123) has paid particular

Its use was not confined to the Christians; for in the sepulchres of the Villa Corsina, near Rome, there are some examples, some of which, it is true, have the *solium* occupied by cinerary urns[1], but in others it is plainly intended for an entire corpse.

It will of course be understood that the difference

attention to the forms and arrangements of sepulchres; for which his professional and scientific studies as a surgeon seem to have given him an especial predilection. In his journey from Tyre to Sidon, he explored the tombs, represented in figs. X, Y, Z. He describes them as an extensive series of catacombs, cut in the face of the white sandstone rock. His view of the interior of one of these chambers exactly corresponds to Mr Scoles' architectural drawings; but Mr Wilde says, "The moment I entered the first of these tombs (exhibited in the engraving), I was struck not only with the resemblance, but the exact similarity they bore to the Egyptian catacombs, especially to those of Sackara and Alexandria. Like them, they have a low square doorway, opening into a chamber, varying in size from ten to fifteen feet square, containing three horizontal sarcophagi, or places for bodies, one on each side; the doorway, or entrance, fills up the fourth side, the whole carved out of the solid rock, which like that of Egypt is soft, and easily excavated." Of the catacombs of Sackara he says, "This tomb, to which the Arabs give the name of Bergami, is one of vast extent and matchless elegance of design and finish; all carved with the greatest precision out of the solid rock. Its outer hall or apartment is of great size, and adorned with massive pillars on either hand. Off the sides of this portion of the tomb are a series of small chambers, their walls covered with hieroglyphics: in form they are for the most part square, and have in general three niches for the bodies; one opposite to the door, and one on either side. Two square wells lead down to a great depth into a lower tier of sepulchral chambers, similarly coated with phonetic writing." (Vol. I. p. 372.) Upon comparing the accounts of different travellers and writers, I cannot, however, satisfy myself how far the similarity of the Egyptian loculus to the Syrian is to be interpreted. The question respecting which I should be exceedingly grateful for exact information is this: Does the Arcosolium, in its exact form and arched opening, as in the Christian catacombs of Rome, and in the Syrian tomb of the above woodcuts, exist in the tombs of Egypt? Vide Wilkinson, Manners and Customs, Vol. II. 2nd series, p. 397; Pococke, Vol. I. p. 54; Clarke, Vol. III. p. 286, 4to edition. Clarke says distinctly of the small chambers of the Alexandrian catacomb, that "each contains on either side of it, except that of the entrance, a *soros* for the reception of a mummy:" these chambers are about nine feet square.

[1] See Bartoli, Ant. Sepolcri, tav. 9, 11, 13.

between the *arcosolium* and a sarcophagus placed in a niche or isolated, is simply that in the former the *solium* is a part of the structure, very often indeed part of the solid rock, and therefore it shews its front only; but the sarcophagus is an isolated chest, and often moveable, and has three finished sides at least, and when not placed against the wall, is ornamented on four sides.

The arcosolium is plainly the prototype of the mediæval monuments that are constructed in the side-walls of churches.

In the Etruscan sepulchres there is no example of a genuine "arcosolium." When a sarcophagus is employed, it is always placed against the walls of the apartment, or isolated, but never fitted into a recess either arched or square, and the same may be said of the stone-couches. But recesses, both arched and rectangular, without the hollow chest, are sunk in the sides of the Etruscan chambers, and in the vertical faces of rock, for the reception of bodies[2].

---

[2] The descriptions which travellers give (without drawings) are so ambiguous, that I cannot affirm that the recess always occurs in the Jewish tombs. Schultz seems to imply this in the description I have quoted above, in which case he must be supposed to mean that the tombs near Jerusalem in which the recess does not occur, belonged to foreigners. Doubdan, in the following passage, clearly states that the body was either deposited in a stone chest, sufficiently deep to admit of a horizontal cover, or else simply laid upon the surface of a kind of altar left in the rock, and hollowed about an inch. But he says nothing about the recess in the floor of which these receptacles were formed; and similarly Clarke, Vol. II. p. 252, 4to edition, comparing the tombs of Telmessus with those of the Hill of Offence, south of Jerusalem, is equally ambiguous. I must leave this question to be answered by actual observers; for as the tombs of Asia Minor are of both kinds, as already stated, it is impossible to say which he alludes to. The drawing of one of these tombs in the Hill of Offence, which is given by Zuallardo, and copied by Cotovicus, represents a simple rectangular loculus, hollowed in the side of the apartment, like those of the ordinary Christians in the Roman catacombs. But more of this below.

"Some of these tombs (on the

Besides the ordinary kinds of single chambers which Schultz has explained, there are at Jerusalem many of a more complicated and remarkable construction, which have been described with more or less precision by travellers. They resemble the simple chambers in the forms of their receptacles (or *loculi*) for the dead, and differ from them only in consisting of a number of apartments connected in various ways by passages and staircases, instead of having merely a single chamber with its vestibule; and they are moreover distinguished by an ornamental façade of architecture, the style of which is, in them all, Greek, and often with a strange intermixture of Egyptian principles, the

---

North of Jerusalem) consist of simple low-arched grottos, of an oblong form, leading from the antechambers. There are also others similar to those of Telmessus, Laodicea and Tortosa, having ledges at the sides; and again, others having niches for the bodies, representing the segment of a dome (arch ?) like those in the royal sepulchres, (Tombs of the Kings)." Wilde, Vol. II. p. 308. Of the southern tombs, however, namely, those on the Mountain of Offence, mentioned by Clarke, with the Greek inscriptions, Mr Wilde (Vol. II. p. 336) says they invariably correspond to the type of the eastern tomb, having *horizontal benches* for the bodies ranged along the sides.

"Les Juifs, au moins les plus riches et considerables, avoient coustume de choisir dès leur vivant le lieu de leur sepulture, qui estoit pour l'ordinaire un petit cabinet ou caveau, qu'ils faisoient tailler à la pointe du ciseau dans quelque roche vive, de la grandeur d'un corps de six à sept pieds en quarré, et l'entrée fort petite. Dans ce caveau ou cabinet ils faisoient tailler à costé et de la mesme roche un cercueil, creusé avec un petit relais à un bout, pour hausser un peu la teste, de la mesme longueur de six à sept pieds, et environ deux de largeur, où ayant mis le corps mort enveloppé de son suaire et couvert d'une table de pierre, ils bouchoient la porte d'une autre grande pierre qu'ils faisoient sceller avec du ciment, et l'appuyoient avec une autre plus petite.

"Les autres se contentoient, au lieu de cercueil, de laisser un banc de la mesme roche en forme d'autel, creusé seulement d'un poulce, sur le quel on estendoit le corps, sans etre couvert d'une autre pierre. Voilà la forme de la plus grande partie des sepulchres de ce pays-là, et particulièrement de celuy de Nostre Seigneur," &c. Doubdan, le Voyage de la Terre Sainte, p. 65, 2nd ed. 1661. (He began his travels Nov. 25th, 1651.)

exact period of which it is by no means easy to determine. The names given to many of these larger sepulchres have plainly no authority, such as, the Tombs of the Prophets, of the Judges, of the apostle James, and of Jehoshaphat[1] and others.

The tombs so distinguished by names, are not the only ones of this kind near Jerusalem. Robinson (for example) describes another in a state of decay, at some distance S.E. of the Tombs of the Kings, and states that several others of a similar character may be traced[2].

For the elucidation of my subject, I shall venture to lay before my readers a description of two of the larger class of tombs, namely, of the Tomb of the Judges, as a specimen of the excavated catacomb; and of the Tomb of Absalom as a monolith.

---

[1] Plans and drawings of the Tombs of the Kings may be found in various works. Mr Wilde (Vol. II. p. 300) has described them at length, and with some particulars omitted by other travellers. "There are no troughs or soroi in any of the chambers of this subterranean mausoleum, but simply ledges or sides like those of the regal sepulchres in Asia Minor." He proceeds to describe minutely the sarcophagi. The best plan appears to be that of Catherwood, which is published in Robinson, Vol. I. p. 530. Cassas gives plans and sections, which, compared with those of more recent travellers, appear to be sadly dressed up from very scanty and inaccurate notes. See also Bartlett, p. 129, and most of the picturesque works on Jerusalem. Cassas has also given plans of the tombs of the apostle James and of Jehosaphat; but I regret to say that these drawings of Cassas exhibit every symptom of having been made up from very hasty sketches. A plan and description of the tombs of the prophets is given by Lord Nugent, in his "Lands Classical and Sacred." Shaw describes the rock-sepulchres of *Latikea* (the ancient Laodicea), and adds that those near Jebilee, Tortosa, and the Serpent Fountain, together with those that are commonly called the Royal Sepulchres at Jerusalem,...are of the like workmanship and contrivance with the *crypta* of *Latikea* (Shaw's Travels, Second Ed. p. 263). Consult also "Agincourt, Histoire de l'Art par les Monuments."

[2] Bib. Res. Vol. I. p. 534.

IV.

THE TOMBS OF THE JUDGES.

THE remarkable catacomb which is known by the name of the Tombs of the Judges, is an excellent example of the various modes in which the niches, or places of deposit for the dead, were arranged, when a considerable number were to be provided for, and a series of chambers formed with due regard to symmetry.

The kindness of my friend, Mr Scoles, to whom I have so often had the pleasure of referring in these pages, has enabled me to lay before my readers his complete architectural elucidation of this *hypogeum*, which, as far as I know, has never been attempted before, although the tomb itself is commonly referred to.

Plate 4 contains a plan and two sections which will completely explain the whole[1].

[1] Fig. 12 is a vertical section of the whole, from West to East, and it shews that there are two floors in the eastern portion.

In fig. 13, which is a general plan, the lower floor is laid down in dotted lines, and the section in fig. 12 is taken in the centre of the upper plan along the line A, B, D, while the section of the lower chambers is taken also along their central line E...K, which is necessarily considerably to the North of the sectional line of the upper chambers.

Fig. 14 is a transverse section of the principal chamber B, and its southern chamber C, taken from North to South. The same letters of reference are employed in all the figures.

Mr Wilde (Vol. II. p. 306) describes a tomb which appears to be the one in question. He tells us that each of the deep *loculi* is slightly arched at top, as Mr Scoles' drawing shews, and adds that each has a square groove hewn in the rock round the entrance of it, for the reception of a door. They are more probably for a single slab to be cemented against the front of it. These square sinkings are indicated in the drawings.

"The bodies must have been put into these holes without any coffins... I would say that, from the appearance presented by the hewn surface, the rock was first roughly cut with an instrument in the form of a pick, with a flattened point, and then smoothed by

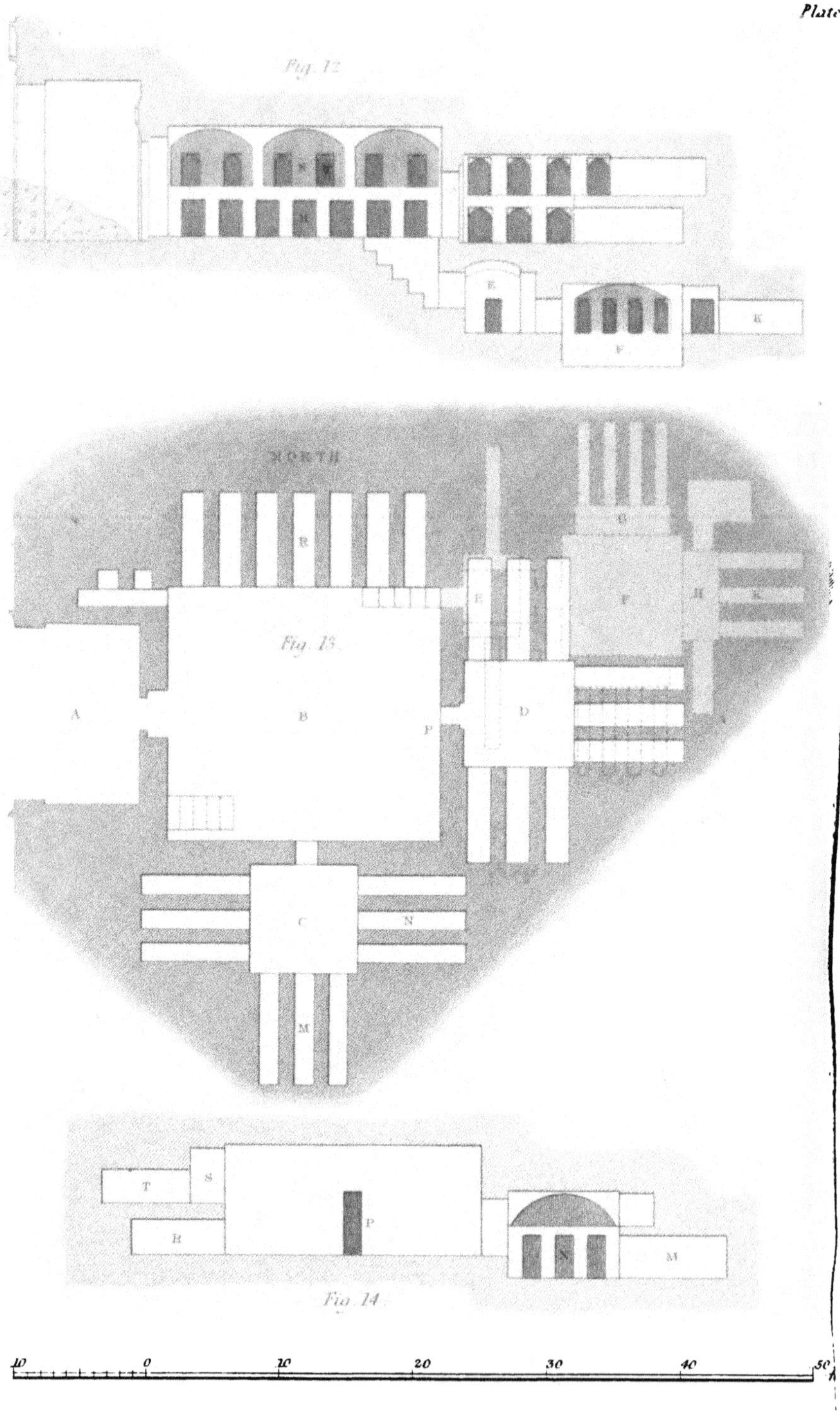

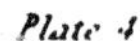

Fig. 12

E
F
K

NORTH

R
E
D
F
H
K
Fig. 13
A
B
P
D
C
N
M

T
S
R
P
N
M

Fig. 14

10 0 10 20 30 40 50

TOMBS OF THE JUDGES.

J. J. Scoles del. Novr 1825

J.W.Lo

The entrance faces the West[2], and has a vestibule (A) thirteen feet by nine feet, the opening of which is equal in width and height to the vestibule itself, and is ornamented with a simple architrave moulding surmounted by a Greek-looking pediment having *acroteria* at the corners and in the centre. Within is a small door of narrow proportions[3], also decorated with an architrave and pediment.

This door opens to a chamber (B) very nearly square, twenty feet in depth, nineteen across from North to South, and eight feet one inch in height. Its ceiling is perfectly flat.

The North side is seen (in elevation) in fig. 12. It is occupied by two tiers of receptacles or *loculi*, the section of which is shewn on the left hand of the transverse section, fig. 14. These drawings will shew that the lower tier consists of seven plain cavities excavated in the rock, on the level of the floor, and perpendicularly to the side of the room, and each seven feet in length, two feet nine inches in height, and one foot eight inches wide. The upper tier is formed of three arched recesses, the floors of which are raised three feet nine inches above that of the room. Their arch is segmental, and they are two feet six inches deep, so that each of them would receive either a swathed corpse or a small sarcophagus.

The back of each recess is also pierced by two deep *loculi* rather narrower than those below, but in other

---

some fine-grained tool, like a comb-pointed chisel. A similar appearance is exhibited on some of the rocks out of which are formed the sepulchral chambers in Egypt." Wilde, Vol. II. p. 308.

[2] This entrance is engraved by Cassas, (with some inaccuracies) under the title of Tomb of the Kings of Judah, and his representation is copied in the Pictorial Bible, and in Kitto's Pictorial Sunday-Book, No. 932.

[3] 6′.9″ high and 2′.5″ wide.

respects similar. Thus it appears that this system unites the two methods of depositing the body which, as already stated, are usually employed in this neighbourhood, namely, the long and shallow loculus with a raised floor, upon which the body was laid parallel to the side of the room, and the narrow and deep loculus in which it was laid at right angles to the side of the room.

This room (with the exception of a deep loculus opening to some smaller ones which are seen in the North-West corner,) contains no other receptacle. But in the middle of its South and of its East side is a narrow door[1], each leading to a room about eight feet square, and containing (as the plan shews) three deep loculi on each of three sides. But these two rooms differ in other respects. The Southern room, the floor of which is two feet lower than that of the great room, is shewn in section at the right end of fig. 14. This section also exhibits an elevation of the eastern side of the room; and as the southern and eastern sides of the room are arranged in exactly the same manner, the section of the southern side, compared with the elevation of the eastern which is close to it, completely explains the forms and depths of the loculi. The lower ones, three on a side, are similar in form and dimension to those of the great room. Above them is an arched receptacle of the same depth as those of the great room, but it is lower, and has no deep loculi pierced at its back. The room itself is only six feet six inches high.

The Eastern room D, is arranged in a totally different manner as far as its upper loculi are concerned;

---

[1] 4′. 8″ high, 1′. 6″ wide.

but as its dimensions are about the same as those of the Southern room C, and its lower loculi arranged in the same manner, three on a side, the two rooms appear exactly alike on the plan[2].

But the section of the Eastern room (fig. 1) shews that at the level of the upper loculi the sides of the room are set back[3] two feet nine inches, so as to allow space for four loculi instead of three on each side, in addition to the space in front, which may be supposed also to have been intended for the reception of bodies laid parallel to the walls, as in the arched recesses of the upper tier in the rooms already described.

It remains only to describe the lower floor, of which the plan is shewn in dotted lines in fig. 13, and the section in fig. 12. In the North-east corner of the great room B, a staircase leads down to a small vestibule E, which has more of architectural arrangement about it than any other apartment of this catacomb; for there is a sunk recess on three of its sides, headed by a segmental arch which reaches to the top of the room, and the ceiling springs from these arches in a slightly domical form, every other apartment in the catacomb being flat-roofed. These recesses are solely intended for ornament, for they are too shallow and too small to receive bodies, being only a foot in depth and four feet long, and the apartment itself including them is but six feet across, and about five feet high.

---

[2] The loculi of the South room are 1′. 4″ wide, 8′. 1″ deep, and 3′. 3″ high, and those of the West room 1′. 10″ wide, 8′. 2″ deep, and 2′. 6″ high.

[3] The section only shews this setting back on the eastern side of the room, but the same contrivance is adopted on the North and on the South sides of the room, so that there are four loculi in the upper tier of each side, making, in addition to those below, twenty-one loculi in this apartment. The floor of the upper tier is only 3′. 5″ above the floor of the room.

The north and south sides have each one opening communicating with a deep narrow loculus. Its east side has a low door, only two feet six high, which opens to the sepulchral chamber F. The floor of the sepulchral chamber is two feet six inches below the sill of this door, and similarly the floor of the vestibule is two feet three inches below the sill of its door of entrance.

In this sepulchral chamber another mode of distribution is adopted, for there is but one tier of loculi. The chamber (eight feet ten inches square, and six feet two inches high), has on each of three sides an arched recess (G, H) forming a loculus of the shallow kind, the bottom of which is two feet six inches from the floor of the chamber. The back of each is pierced with three or with four deep narrow loculi, as in the first chamber B.

The eastern arch A, has also, as the plan shews, sepulchral recesses pierced on its north and south sides.

This lower story appears to be a complete sepulchre in itself, having its own vestibule. It is very well worth observation, that of the four principal chambers of this catacomb no two are arranged precisely in the same manner, and that great pains appear to have been taken to distribute the loculi with regard to symmetry and variety in design. Whether the arched recesses of the upper tiers were intended for the reception of bodies or for sarcophagi it is difficult to say, but they appear too short for sarcophagi.

The staircase in the south-western corner of the principal apartment B, leads down to an unfinished excavation.

V.

THE TOMB OF ABSALOM.

To complete this sketch of the Jewish sepulchres, I must advert to the isolated tombs, known by the names of Absalom and Zachariah, which are placed on the east side of Jerusalem, immediately opposite to the southern extremity of the Temple Area, as shewn in the general plan of the town. They are, in the words of the accurate Robinson, "situated in the narrowest part of the Valley of Jehosaphat, where a shelf, or ledge of rock, extends down from the East, and terminates in an almost perpendicular face just over the bed of the Kidron." The Tomb of Zachariah is on the South, and that of Absalom about 200 feet to the North of it, and slightly westward. Each tomb is square, and stands North and South. The drawings will completely explain the tomb of Absalom, at least as far as it rises above the ground, for its lower part is now buried to a considerable height in a mass of débris and of stones, which have been cast at it by the Jews, who, believing it to be really the Pillar of Absalom, (mentioned in 2 Samuel xviii. 18), have been in the habit, from time immemorial, of shewing their horror at his rebellious conduct by casting a stone and spitting as they pass by it[1].

The lower part, however, is a mass of solid rock about twenty feet square, which has been completely detached from the cliff behind it, by working away a passage ten feet in width at the sides, and nine at the back, so as to leave the tomb standing in a square recess hewn out of the cliff, as shewn in the plan and in the section. This square mass has a pilaster at each

[1] Holy City, p. 375, 1st Edit.

angle, and a quarter column attached to it, and also two half columns between; these columns have Ionic capitals, and the pilasters Greek-looking antæ-capitals. Their bases are buried in the rubbish. They sustain an entablature of a singularly mixed character; its frieze and architrave are Doric and have triglyphs and guttæ. The metope is occupied by a circular disk or shield. But in lieu of the regular cornice, there is one which resembles the Egyptian cornice, consisting of a deep and high cavetto, and a bold torus below it. The exact altitude of this lower story cannot be ascertained for want of excavation, but Mr Scoles estimates it at about twenty-five feet; above it is a *square* attic, rather more than seven feet in height, and surmounted by a simple cornice.

Upon this again is placed a *circular* attic, and the whole is finished by a peculiarly formed roof, which is exactly delineated in Plates 5 and 6, as well as the profiles and details of the architecture.

The parts above the Egyptian cornice are built of masonry, but below that line the whole is worked out of one piece of rock. The four fronts are of the same size and design, but the front towards the city is better executed than the others.

In the rocky part a chamber is formed, of which the plan and section is given in the drawings, as far as Mr Scoles could ascertain them; the lower part of the chamber being unfortunately so encumbered with rubbish, and with the stones that have been thrown into it, that its lower arrangements and altitude cannot be made out. It is not quite eight feet square, is placed nearer to the South side than to the others, by which room is obtained for arched recesses on the North and West. On the East, a low door immediately above the cornice gives access to a stair of entrance. The thickness would admit of an arched recess on this side, but if it exist, it must be lower than the others and entirely concealed by the rubbish. The ceiling of the chamber is flat, and decorated with an ornamental panel, and a Greek moulding as a cornice. The obstructed state of the lower part makes it impossible to see whether there be any provision for the reception of the dead in the recesses, which, to judge by the upper parts, are deep enough to receive a body; the northern one being two feet three inches. It is probable, from the usual lowness of these sepulchral chambers, that another apartment exists below this with a more ample entrance, if indeed this entrance has not been walled up. In the chamber that remains above-ground there is no apparent means of introducing a dead body, much less a sarcophagus.

But my principal reason for introducing this monument, besides the pleasure of presenting to the public, for the first time, these accurate drawings of Mr Scoles, is, that it affords to us, close to the walls of Jerusalem, an example of the very system which appears to have been pursued by the architects of Constantine in the decoration of the Holy Sepulchre; with this difference, that in the latter case, the cave had existed for centuries before they began their external operations; whereas in the former case, the chamber and the external form were probably parts of one design. Moreover, Constantine clothed the rock with an artificial casing of rich marble, and in our present example, the ornaments are worked out of the solid limestone. But they each exhibit an example of the detaching of a complete monolithic representation of a structure, by the levelling away of the original rock on all sides. The unmerciful ridicule and contempt which has been cast upon those who have ventured to suppose such a process possible, in the case of the Holy Sepulchre, is at once disposed of, by thus shewing that examples of this process exist in the immediate neighbourhood of Jerusalem; for the tomb of Zachariah is exactly formed in the same manner. And whatever may be the age of these works, they certainly are prior to the time of Constantine. But away from Jerusalem there are many examples, especially in Asia Minor[1]. Robinson also found "several isolated monuments, the counterparts of the monolithic tombs in the Valley of Jehoshaphat" at Petra[2].

VI.

DESCRIPTION OF THE HOLY SEPULCHRE.

The Holy Sepulchre itself is in its present state, as I have already stated, a small chapel or edicula in the centre of the Rotunda, about twenty-six feet long and eighteen broad. As the diameter of the interior of the Rotunda is sixty-seven feet, the chapel stands quite free in the midst of it.

The Eastern end is square, and the Western polygonal. The external aspect of it has been completely altered by the repairs that followed the fire of 1808; for the original exterior casing of marble, greatly damaged by that fire, has been of necessity entirely removed, and a new one substituted of a totally dif-

[1] Vide especially Texier, Pls. 197, 198, for a monolithic tomb, detatched from the rock precisely in the same manner as that of Absalom, and wrought into the form of a Doric temple.

[2] Robinson, Vol. I. p. 521. They are sketched in one of Roberts's views of the Necropolis of Petra.

ferent design. The comparison of its present plan with that of its former state proves also, that at least the Eastern half of it has been completely rebuilt, so as also to change the interior[1].

But, in fact, the interior of the Chapel is divided into two apartments. The only entrance is at the East, where a small door admits to the first apartment, which is called the Chapel of the Angel; for here, as they say, the Angel sat upon the stone that was rolled from the door of the Sepulchre. And, accordingly, a stone about a foot high and two feet square is exhibited in this Chapel, as the identical stone in question, or rather as a piece of it.

At the Western extremity of the Angel's Chapel, a narrow low door opens to the second or inner apartment, which is the Sepulchre itself, a quadrangular room, about six feet by seven, and eight or nine feet in height.

This inner apartment is asserted to be the original

---

[1] Figs. 6, 7, 8, Plate 2, shew the Chapel of the Sepulchre, as it has appeared at different periods; Fig. 6, the supposed original arrangement of Constantine; Fig. 7, is that of the Crusaders, as given by Bernardino and as it remained until 1808. Fig. 8 is its present plan; for which I am indebted to Mr Scoles.

In these three figures the same letters of reference are used: A, the altar of the Sepulchre, B the rock-chamber, C the low door, D the Chapel of the Angel, having the *stone* in the midst, EE stone benches, FF candelabra introduced into the present structure, G a platform of approach to the Sepulchre, raised three steps above the floor of the rotunda, H the Chapel of the Copts.

The probable rocky part of the structure is distinguished from the masonry and marble covering by different shading. In Fig. 6, the sepulchral chamber, not having been lined with marble, appears larger than in the others. In Fig. 8 a narrow staircase is shewn to the right and left of the entrance of the Angel Chapel, which serves to give access to the roof. For this information I am indebted to a Russian plan. It is probable that a similar staircase existed in the earlier building, although Bernardino has omitted it.

Rock-cave, which was shaped and pared down on the outside by Constantine's architect, and the surface of the rock levelled all round it, so as to leave it standing up in the midst, like an artificial construction. The outside was then also decorated with a marble casing and with columns, which casing has been destroyed and reconstructed in various forms, until it has assumed its present appearance. As for the Angel's Chapel in front of it, it is confessedly a building of stone, and has never been described as a rock-cavern, like the inner room, by any writer of authority, although some travellers have assumed this, and perhaps the inferior priests who shew the Sepulchre may say so. But in examining the traditional accounts of the whole of these buildings, and the pretences that are put forth by their guardians with respect to them, it is quite necessary to confine ourselves to the writings of educated men. The marvellous tales of the priests who shew the wonders of the spot to the pilgrims, are about as worthy of attention as the histories that are delivered by a Cathedral verger in our own country, some of which are nearly as preposterous as the legends of the Holy Land, although not so revolting, because the subjects of them are not so sacred.

The wood-cut at the beginning of this volume shews its present appearance, which is that of a Russo-Greek Chapel, in a very bad taste, surmounted by a swelled dome, of a form, happily, peculiar to the Russian Churches. In the drawings of Breydenbach, and others from his time down to the fire of 1808, the Western part of the Chapel has a simple arcade against its sides, the columns of which are seen in the Plan, Fig. 7, from which it appears that there were nine arches. These arches are not only drawn as pointed arches by Bernardino (who very rarely represents pointed arches,) but he mentions one of them expressly (that over the Eastern door) as a pointed arch, "*arco ottuso.*" (p. 44). But Breydenbach, Le Brun, and others, draw them as semicircular arches. Nevertheless I incline to think, that the fact of one observer drawing the arches in the pointed form, is conclusive against all the others, who might so probably have missed that peculiarity at a period when the pointed arch had not been made an object of attention. The columns, as Bernardino tells us, were different in diameter and in form; some were cylindrical, some octagonal, some spiral, and their plinths were of different heights, as if they had been taken from the remains of other structures. The arcade only extended from K to K Westward, and the height of this part of the Chapel was little more than fifteen feet[1], and was surmounted by a single cornice. The part to the Eastward of KK was a foot lower, and had a similar cornice. The Eastern face contained the only door, and this was square-headed, but had a pointed arch or pannel over it, sunk a few inches. A platform G nine feet wide, shewn in the plan, and raised about a foot above the general pavement of the Rotunda, led to this door, and there was a stone seat E on either side of the doorway. The Eastern half of the Chapel has been now wholly rebuilt, and the Western re-cased, so as to alter its appearance entirely, and to increase its height. But this arrangement of the platform and seats has been preserved, as the plan, Fig. 8, shews, although they have been constructed in a more com-

[1] Twenty-one palms, (Bernardino, p. 44.)

modious and handsome form, and the platform is also now flanked by two large candlesticks at FF. But to return to Fig. 7, or to the Chapel at the period of that plan. The Western half was surmounted by a light pavilion, erected over the sepulchral chamber. This consisted of a plinth of white marble, on which were placed twelve small columns in pairs, of the finest porphyry, with white marble bases and capitals of metal, of irregular design, (according to Bernardino, which may be rendered as applying to mediæval work). Upon these stood six pointed arches of wood, and a cornice of multiplied mouldings, capped by a cupola of lead. This little fabric, nineteen feet high in all, and eleven in diameter, appears to have been of exceedingly mean design and disproportionately small dimensions, though perhaps scarcely deserving Dr Clarke's epithet of a "dusty pepper-box." The present dumpy dome which replaces it, is not worth much more consideration.

The original Angel Chapel was, as the plan (Fig. 7) shews, a small parallelogram, ten feet by five, with a semicircular apse to the West. The parallelogram was vaulted with a groined vault, the apex of which was only ten feet from the floor, and the apse was still lower. The Eastern door was eight feet five inches to the crown of its pointed arch, but the Western door, which gave admission to the inner or sepulchral chamber, was only three feet four inches in height, and the passage was cut obliquely on account of the arrangements of the Sepulchre within[1]. Its pavement and its walls were covered and lined with marble, and there were two small windows on either side, and an *ambry* in which

[1] The above measures are reduced from Bernardino's palms.

were kept some of the sacred vessels for the service of the Sepulchre[2].

The present Angel Chapel (D, Fig. 8) is an entirely new structure, of slightly increased dimensions, and of a different form. The principal interest of comparing the two plans, is to prove that the apse of the old one was certainly no part of the rock; for the present chamber completely encroaches upon that apse, and it is not likely that the rock itself would have been meddled with by the modern architect, if he had found it in his way. In the middle of the Chapel is fixed the stone whereon the Angel sat, upon which it is scarcely worth while to waste words, as it has been repeatedly changed. It is, manifestly, only a representation even of the one which Bede alludes to, as will be shewn below[3].

The inner apartment, or Cave of the Sepulchre, was not affected by the fire of 1808. It is a four-sided chamber very nearly square, six feet eight inches English in length, and six feet one inch in width, according to Mr Scoles. Its vault is eight feet six from the floor. More than half of this chamber on the North side is occupied by a kind of altar or pedestal, two feet ten inches in height, which covers and protects the real Sepulchral couch, where the body of our

[2] Quaresmius, Tom. II. p. 510, and Cotovicus.

[3] "The stone which now stands in the ante-room of the tomb, and which is set forth to be the great stone that was rolled to the door of the Sepulchre...is a square block of white marble, yet the holy fathers declare this to be the identical stone; and it is exhibited as a costly spectacle, and kissed, and venerated accordingly. When strictly questioned on the subject, however, the guide informed us that the true stone was stolen by the Armenians, and it is exhibited by them in a chapel that occupies the site of the palace of Caiaphas, on Mount Zion, but that the polished block of marble served their purpose equally well." Richardson, Vol. II. p. 335.

Lord was laid. The entrance to the chamber is on the East, and close to the side of this altar.

The sides of the chamber are not exactly at right angles to each other; its North-Eastern and North-Western angles being slightly acute, and the others the reverse, according to Bernardino's plan, and to his verbal description quoted below[1].

The chamber is asserted to be hewn out of a rock, but its surface is so covered with ornamental decoration, and blackened with the smoke of the lamps which are continually kept burning therein, that no part of the rocky surface appears to be visible[2]. Quaresmius, who is certainly not inclined to weaken or withhold evidence, and would have mentioned the rock if he could, says that the sides of the chamber within and without are clothed with squared slabs of marble of an ash colour, and the roof incrusted with rough mortar; but that he doubts not that it was once covered with the most elegant Mosaic work[3], of which traces and remains might be still seen, as far as the thick black smoke

---

[1] "Il vano del S. Sepolcro è per li suoi angoli acuti et ottusi pal. otto e mezo lungo, e otto larga..." p. 32. "Il S. Sepolcro è quattro palmi, e di quì alla volta sono otto; talche in tutto sono palmi dodici, e la porta è quattro palmi e mezo." Bernardino, p. 44. In Mr Scoles' plan (Fig. 8) this peculiarity is omitted; but that gentleman informs me that he thinks it probable it may exist, and that it may have escaped his observation.

[2] Cotovicus, for example, says the interior surface of the cave is hidden by its marble covering, and as for the roof, the smoke of the fifty lamps, which burn there day and night, has so obscured it, that no one can tell whether it be rock, or plaster, or marble covering. p. 180. F. Fabri however, in 1483, declares that he found rocky surface exposed about the door of the cavern, (see the next section below).

[3] Quaresmius, p. 504. Baldensel, in 1336, testifies to the existence of these ornaments, in his description of the sepulchre, the "parvula domuncula," into which, on account of the lowness of the door, which is to the East, it is necessary to stoop in entering. Above, it is vaulted in a semicircular form, and decorated with mosaic work, and with gold and marble, having no window. Canisii Thes. Tom. IV. p. 349.

of the lamps would allow. As to the Holy Sarcophagus itself, he informs us that it was covered with white marble slabs[4], by Father Bonifacius (A.D. 1555), after much consideration, in order to protect this sacred tomb from the droppings of lamp-oil and other uncleanness, and from the indiscreet zeal of the faithful, who were continually knocking off small particles to carry away. The upper slab was in one piece, but was marked across to make it appear as if broken, to deceive the Turks, who would certainly have appropriated so beautiful a piece of marble, if they had seen it entire[5]. It is used as an altar for daily mass. This is Quaresmius' account, and it is worth remarking, because it proves that the best informed writers do not pretend that the altar, which is shewn as the Sepulchre, is the real tomb, but only that it covers the real tomb[6]. What the form of the Sepulchre beneath really is, or was, is a curious subject of enquiry, which we shall presently examine. The inner chamber remains now much in the same state as it did before the fire of 1808; unless, indeed, the decorations have been renewed or repaired, which, comparing the plans, Figs. 7, 8, appears to be the case.

Modern travellers are too apt to assume that the altar exhibited in the inner chamber is asserted to be the original Sepulchre; and probably the priests who shew the wonders of the place, are not very careful to

[4] It will be shewn in the next section, that the sepulchre was covered with marble for the first time, after the destruction of the church by the Caliph Hakem, and that the covering by Father Bonifacius was a mere repair.

[5] Quaresmius, p. 510; also Wilde's Madeira, Vol. II. p. 295; and Schultz, Jerusalem, p. 98.

[6] Cotovicus similarly tells us, that a marble altar occupies the greater part of the chamber on the North, and contains, shut up within it, the place where the Lord's body rested, "altare marmoreum id verò locum quo Christi corpus jacuit sepultum...occlusum continet." p. 181.

explain this, if they themselves are even aware of its history. But the effect of their exhibiting an altar, which is plainly a construction of marble slabs, as the representation of a tomb which we have the words of Holy Writ to assure us was hewn out of the solid rock, is, and always has been, to provoke incredulity, censure, and doubts as to the genuineness of the spot itself. William de Baldensel, a traveller, even so early as A. D. 1336, describes the "domuncula" or chapel in question, and the place of the Lord's Sepulchre, on the right hand. But he adds, that "it must be remarked, that the monument placed over that most holy spot is not the very one in which the sacred Body was originally laid, for *that*, according to holy Scripture, was hewn out of the living rock; even as many monuments of the ancients, and especially those in the neighbourhood, were formed. But *this* is made of numerous stones, put together with fresh mortar, and very rudely, so as to appear scarcely decent[1]." He then goes on to account for this

[1] "...In medio Ecclesiæ parvula domuncula est, in quam propter portæ demissionem versus Orientem, intrare oportet corpore incurvato: supra verò testudinata est ad modum semicirculi, opere Mosaico, auro et marmoribus deornata, nullam habens fenestram, candelis lampade illustrata. In hujus domunculæ parte dextra locus est Dominicæ Sepulturæ, attingens extremitates prædictæ casæ in longum, scilicet ab Oriente versus Occidentem, cujus longitudo novem communium palmarum est, latitudo verò tam *monumenti*, quam spacii cæteri ipsius domunculæ residuum, in latitudine circa sex palmas communes utrobique se extendit; circa 12 palmas potest esse altitudo domunculæ supradictæ. Illud verò advertendum est, quod *monumentum* illi sanctissimo loco superpositum, non est illud, in quo corpus Christi sacratissimum exanime primitùs est immissum; quia, sacro attestante eloquio, monumentum Christi erat excisum in petra viva, scilicet, quomodo antiquorum monumenta, et præcipuè in his partibus fieri communiter consueverunt; illud verò ex petris pluribus est compositum, de novo conglutinato cæmento, minus artificialiter et minus quàm deceat, ordinatè...Veruntamen quicquid sit de hoc, ipse locus sepulchri Christi formaliter moveri non potest, sed remansit et remanebit immobilis in æternum." Guilielmi de Baldensel, Hodœporicon ad Terram Sanctam. A. D. 1336. Canis. Thes. Tom. IV. p. 348. From the man-

in his own way, by saying that if any part of the original monument had remained, the Christians never would have abandoned the spot to the Pagans, and so on; and that, after all, if the Sepulchre be gone, the place where it stood can never be moved.

Clarke visited Jerusalem in 1801, therefore before the fire. He relates that "there are no remains whatsoever of any ancient known Sepulchre, that with the most attentive and scrupulous examination he could possibly discover. The sides of the chamber consist of thick slabs of that beautiful breccia vulgarly called verd-antique marble, and over the entrance, which is rugged and broken owing to the pieces carried off as relics, the substance is of the same nature[2]."

Richardson, a very intelligent describer, who visited the Church in 1822, states that "the tomb exhibited is a sarcophagus of white marble, slightly tinged with blue, six feet one inch and three quarters long, three feet three quarters of an inch broad, and two feet one inch and a quarter deep, measured on the outside. It is but indifferently polished, and seems as if it had been at one time exposed to the pelting of the storm, &c.... The sarcophagus occupies about one half of the sepulchral chamber, and extends from one end of it to the other. A space about three feet wide in front of it, is all that remains for the reception of visitors, so that not above three or four can be admitted at a time[3]."

The North side above the altar or tomb was occu-

---

ner in which the word *monumentum* is used (which I have marked in Italics), it is plain that he employs it for the altar or loculus only, and does not intend to apply it to the entire sepulchral chamber.

[2] Clarke's Travels, 4to. Vol. II. p. 544.

[3] Richardson's Travels along the Mediterranean, &c. 1822, Vol. II. p. 322.

pied by a picture representing the Resurrection[1]. In the interior view of the Sepulchre, which Le Brun has engraved, this picture is shewn, and the altar appears detached from the ends of the apartment by a small space; but this is inconsistent with the accounts of other travellers. He shews the roof in the form of a common groined vault, and states that there were forty-four silver lamps kept constantly burning, and all suspended from the roof. Of these lamps thirteen belonged to the Latins, twenty-one to the Greeks, four to the Armenians, and four to the Copts. The smoke was let out by three holes in the vault. And as there was no opening from the chamber but these holes and the little door of entrance, the heat and closeness of the atmosphere were overpowering[2]. At present these openings are replaced by some open work of marble, of the most chaste and elegant workmanship, according to Mr Wilde, who adds, that the top of the chamber is evidently of modern construction, but that the sides of the door as well as the part above it are hewn out of the solid grey limestone-rock, which is there distinctly seen. If this be correct, the marble lining described by Quaresmius and others has been removed since the fire[3].

VII.

THE FORMER STATE AND HISTORY OF THE SEPULCHRE.

COMPARING the above account with the description of the rock-tombs given in the previous sections, it

[1] Zuallardo's and also Le Brun's engravings.

[2] Le Brun. Quaresmius, Tom. II. p. 511.

[3] See Wilde's Madeira, &c. Vol. II. p. 203. He is wrong in saying that the altar was cracked in 1808; Quaresmius has told us it was marked or cracked even in his time to deceive the Turks. See above, p. 167.

must certainly be concluded that the appearance of the Holy Sepulchre at present, and as it existed before 1808, as little resembles a genuine Jewish cave-sepulchre as possible. But it was not always so miserably metamorphosed. If we. trace its history through the writers that mention it from Eusebius downwards, it will appear, that although its exterior was by Constantine's orders disguised under a mask of architectural ornament to do it honour, yet that its interior was reverently left in its original cavern form, and that the present state of the interior is not earlier than the time of the Crusades. I shall have occasion below to refer fully to the principal writers and pilgrims for the explanation of the history of the entire group of buildings around the Sepulchre; but I have thought it best, in the first place, to extract from them all that relates to the Sepulchre itself, in order to keep the history and description of that principal object entirely distinct.

Notwithstanding the importance which Eusebius attaches to the sacred cave, his information with respect to its decoration is very scanty, for he merely says that "the Emperor's magnificence decorated it, as the head of the whole work, with choice columns, and he ornamented it with great care in every possible manner." From the Lectures of St Cyril we learn that the rock was pared and shaped down by the Emperor's orders: "The entrance which was at the door of the Salutary Sepulchre... was hewn out of the rock itself, as is customary here in the front of Sepulchres. Now it appears not; the outer cave or vestibule having been hewn away for the sake of the present adornment; but before the Sepulchre was decorated by royal zeal, there was a cave in the face of the rock." (Lect. xiv.) In another place he appeals to the "stone which was laid at the door of the Sepulchre, which lies to this day by the tomb." (Lect. xiii. 39.) This is all the information which we possess of the state of the Sepulchre from the time of its arrangement by Constantine, to the first attack upon it, which was that made by the Persians, (A. D. 614). But we know, from the innumerable examples that remain, that the practice of both Romans and Greeks was to make the most remarkable of their sepulchral monuments in the form of a small edifice or temple, either wholly constructed of separate stones, or else wholly or partly monolithic.

It was therefore in perfect accordance with their usual habits, that the artists first commissioned to do honour to the Sacred Cave, then a mere excavation in the face of a cliff, should conceive the design of converting it into an isolated *edicula*, and shaping it by paring down the surrounding rock, so as to leave it standing up in a manner that admitted of an architectural casing. We are told that it was decorated with choice columns. From the form of the Western part, it is pretty certain that it was a circular or polygonal building, probably consisting of two stories, in accordance with the usual practice[1].

---

[1] In the plan, Plate 2, Fig. 6, which is a conjectural representation of its state at this period, I have shewn it as decorated with columns in the simplest manner; namely, by converting it into a dodecagonal temple with a peristyle. The West end of the chapel, in Figs. 7 and 8, indicates that the rock was hewn into a portion of a dodecagonal figure. The apse, which appears in its Eastern side, being a classical form, is not improbably a reminiscence of Constantine's architecture, or erected on his foundation, and the number twelve, in accordance with that of the apostles, is also a very probable number to have governed not only the form of the rocky polygon, but also the number of the

The particular effect of the sacking of Jerusalem by the Persians, upon the condition of this little edifice, is not related by the historians. Eutychius, however, informs us that the destruction of the sacred buildings was systematically carried out, and that the Jews in enormous numbers had followed the Persians, to gratify their vengeance against the Christians, by assisting in this work. The Church of the Sepulchre was destroyed by the help of fire, and it is needless to say that it was plundered of its riches, and that the edifice in question must have been reduced to a misshapen and ruined block. In the subsequent restoration by Modestus, it seems to have preserved its character of a little sepulchral chapel. The earliest description of it that follows this restoration[2], is that of Arculfus, (A. D. 697), which is sufficiently

---

columns that surrounded it. Indeed, Eusebius mentions twelve columns, the number of the apostles, as having been placed by Constantine round the apse of the Basilica, as will be seen below.

[2] The credulous narrative of Antoninus Placentinus is of uncertain date, lying between the time of Justinian, whom he mentions, and the Mohammedan conquests, to which he does not allude. But it appears doubtful whether it is to be placed before or after the Persian sack of Jerusalem. His entire description of the buildings about the Sepulchre corresponds in so many particulars with that of Arculfus, that I am inclined to place him after Modestus. His account of the Sepulchre is as follows: "The monument, in which our Lord's body was laid, is hewn out of the natural rock....The stone which closed the Sepulchre still lies before it. The colour of the stone, which was hewn out of Golgotha, cannot be distinguished, for it is ornamented with gold and gems. The rock of the Sepulchre itself is like millstone, and prodigiously decorated with gold and gems, crowns, girdles, belts, and other ornaments suspended from iron rods. The Sepulchre itself is in the fashion of a church, and covered with silver, and before it is placed an altar." This *Itinerarium* is to be found in the Acta Sanctorum. Maii, Tom. II. p. xii.; and in Ugolini Thesau. Tom. VII. I subjoin the original text...."Ingressi sumus in sanctam civitatem, in qua adoravimus Domini monumentum.... Ipsum monumentum, in quo corpus Domini positum fuit, in naturalem excisum est petram. Lucernæ hydria, quæ illo tempore ad caput ejus posita fuerat, ibidem ardet diu noctuque:... Lapis vero, unde clausum fuit monumentum ipsum, est ante illud monumen-

minute, and shews that it then was very different from the chapel in its more modern form. Having described the round church, he proceeds to state that in the middle of it is situated "a round cabin (*tegurium*)[1], cut out of a single piece of rock, within which there is space for *nine men* to stand and pray. The vaulted roof is about a foot and a half above the head of a man of no short stature. The entrance of this little chamber is to the East. The whole of its *exterior surface* is covered with choice marble, and the highest part of its outer roof, ornamented with gold, sustains a golden Cross of no small magnitude. The Sepulchre of the Lord is in the North part of the chamber, and is cut out of the same rock as it, but the pavement of the chamber is lower than the place of sepulture; for there is an altitude of about three palms from the pavement to the lateral edge of the sepulchre.........By the *Sepulchre,* properly so called, is meant that place in the north part of the monumental chamber, in which the Body, wrapped in linen clothes, was deposited, the length of which Arculfus measured with his own hand as seven feet. Which sepulchre is not, as some erroneously imagine, hollowed out into a double form, (*i. e.* in the shape of the body), having a projection left from the solid rock, between and separating the legs and thighs,

---

tum. Color vero pętræ, quæ excisa est de Golgotha (non dignoscitur): nam petra ipsa ornata est auro et gemmis: et postmodum de ipsa petra factum est altare, in loco ubi crucifixus est Dominus. Petra vero monumenti velut molaris est et infinite ornata: virgis ferreis pendent brachialia, dextroceria, (*Dextrocherium,* vide Du Cange, Gloss.) murenæ, monilia, annuli capitulares, cingella, baltei, coronæ, imperium ex auro vel gemmis, et ornamenta plurima. Et ipsum monumentum in modum ecclesiæ coopertum ex argento: et ante monumentum altare positum."

[1] TEGURIUM. Locus seclusus ac superne tectus, a *tegere* voce deducta. Du Cange, Gloss.

but is simple and plain from the head to the feet, and is a couch affording room for one man lying on his back. It is in the manner of a cave, having its opening at the side, and opposite the South part of the monumental chamber. The low roof is artificially wrought above it.

"In this sepulchre twelve lamps, according to the number of the twelve holy Apostles, burn day and night continually, of which four are placed below in the inner part of that sepulchral couch, and the other eight above, over the margin on the right side.........This chamber of the Lord's monument, not being covered within by any ornaments, exhibits to this day the marks of the workmen's tools by which it was excavated. The colour of the rock of the monument and sepulchre is not uniform, but a mixture of red and white[2]."

---

[2] "In medio spatio hujus interioris rotundæ domûs rotundum inest in una eademque petra excisum tegurium, in quo possunt ter terni homines stantes orare, et à vertice alicujus non brevis staturæ stantis hominis, usque ad illius domunculæ cameram, pes et semipes mensura in altum extenditur. Hujus tegurioli introitus ad Orientem respicit, quod totum extrinsecùs electo tegitur marmore, cujus exterius summum culmen auro ornatum, auream non parvam sustentat crucem. In hujus tegurii aquilonali parte sepulchrum Domini in eadem petra interiùs excisum habetur, sed ejusdem tegurii pavimentum humilius est loco sepulchri. Nam à pavimento ejus usque ad sepulchri marginem lateris, quasi trium mensura altitudinis palmorum haberi dignoscitur...

...Sepulchrum verò propriè dicitur ille locus in tegurio, hoc est, in aquilonali parte monumenti, in quo dominicum corpus linteaminibus involutum conditum quievit, cujus longitudinem Arculfus in septem pedum mensura propria mensus est manu.

Quod videlicet sepulchrum non (ut quidam falsò opinantur) duplex est, et quandam de ipsa maceriola petram habens excisam, duo crura et femora duo intercedentem et separantem: sed totum simplex à vertice usque ad plantas, lectum unius hominis capacem super dorsum jacentis præbens spatium in modum speluncæ, introitum à latere habens ad australem partem monumenti è regione respicientem, culmenque humile desuper eminens fabrefactum: in quo utique sepulchro duodenæ lampades, juxta numerum duodecim sanctorum Apostolorum semper die ac nocte ardentes lucent, ex quibus quatuor in imo illius lectuli

He adds, that the stone which was rolled from the mouth of the cave was then broken in two pieces, of which the smaller part, bound with iron, stood in the great Rotunda before the door of the tegurium or chamber, serving for the purposes of an altar, while the larger part, similarly iron-girt, and as an altar, was fixed in the Eastern part of the same Church.

Willibaldus[1], in A. D. 765, describes the Sepulchre

---

sepulcralis loco inferiùs positæ; aliæ vero bis quaternales super marginem ejus superiùs conlocatæ ad latus dexterum, oleo nutriente præfulgent...supradictæ igitur Ecclesiæ formulam, cum rotundo teguriolo in medio ejus conlocato, in cujus aquilonali parte dominicum habetur sepulchrum, subjecta declarat pictura, nec non et trium aliarum figuras ecclesiarum, de quibus inferiùs intimabitur....Sed inter hæc de illo suprà memorato lapide, qui ad ostium monumenti dominici, post ipsius Domini sepultionem crucifixi, multis trudentibus viris advolutus est, breviter intimandum esse videtur. Quem Arculfus intercisum et in duas divisum partes refert; cujus pars minor ferramentis dolata est, et quadratum altare in rotunda supra scripta ecclesia ante ostium sæpe illius memorati tegurii, hoc est dominici monumenti, stans constitutum cernitur: major verò illius lapidis pars æquè circumdolata est, et in Orientali ejusdem Ecclesiæ loco quadrangulum aliud illud altare sub linteaminibus stabilitum extat....Illud dominici monumenti tegurium, nullo intrinsecùs ornatu tectum, usque hodie per totam ejus cavaturam ferramentorum ostendit vestigia, quibus dolatores sive excisores in eodem usi sunt opere: color verò illius ejusdem petræ monumenti et sepulcri, non unus sed duo permixti videntur; ruber utique et albus, inde et bicolor eadem ostenditur petra...." Mabillon, Acta Sanctorum. Sæc. 3. pars 2, p. 504.

[1] "Illud sepulchrum fuerat in petra excisum; et illa petra stat super terram, et est quadrans in imo et in summo subtilis. Et stat nunc in summitate illius sepulchri Crux: et ibi desuper nunc ædificata est mirabilis domus; et in Orientali plaga in illa petra sepulchri est janua, per quam intrant homines in sepulchrum orare. Et ibi est intus lectus, in quo corpus Domini jacebat; et ibi stant in lecto quindecim crateres aurei cum oleo ardentes die noctuque. Ille lectus, in quo corpus Domini jacebat, stat in latere Aquilonis intus in petra Sepulchri; et homini est in dextra manu, quando intrat in sepulchrum orare. Et ibi ante januam sepulchri jacet ille lapis magnus quadrans in similitudinem prioris lapidis quem Angelus revolvit ab ostio monumenti." (Hodœporicon S. Willibaldi, Canisii Thes. Tom. II. p. 111. The "quadrans in imo" refers to the square form of the chamber within, to which Arculfus does not allude, but merely describes the external form of the "tegurium" as round. "In summo subtilis" appears to allude to the pavilion

concisely, adding nothing of importance to the above description; and Bernardus in A. D. 870, refers for the description of the Sepulchre to Bede, who in his tract, "De Locis Sanctis," has merely abridged Arculfus. Epiphanius mentions, but does not describe, the Sepulchre. And these are all the authorities that exist previous to the destruction of the churches by Hakem in A. D. 1010.

It will at once be admitted, that the minute description which Arculfus has given of the interior of the chamber, shews it to have presented a very different appearance from the present one. It was then wholly uncovered in the interior, and exhibited the rocky surface of the cavern, and the sepulchral *loculus* in its original perfection.

Comparing the description of this *loculus* with the various kinds which I have endeavoured to describe in Section III., it must be concluded, that it was an arch-like receptacle sunk in the face of the rock, the bottom of which was either flat or only slightly hollowed as a couch, and its margin raised three palms, or about two feet, above the floor of the chamber. It resembled, in short, the *arco-solium* of figs. X, Y, Z, (Sect. III.) supposing the hollow *solium* to be filled up, so as to leave a level bed for the reception of the body[2]. And this

---

of fine workmanship, which was erected over the Sepulchre, and was surmounted by the Cross.

[2] It is not very clear whether we are to understand from Arculfus that the bottom of the cavity was simply flat like a shelf, or whether a hollow place was sunk into it so as to form a shallow flat-bottomed chest to prevent the body from being displaced, which appears on the whole most probable, for Arculfus only contradicts the assertion that there was a sunk cavity in the shape of a human body. Quaresmius distinctly asserts that the bottom of the Sepulchre was like a chest, large enough to contain a human body, as he was told by those who had seen it when it was laid open (that is, during the repairs of Bonifacius in 1556): "Locus est ad instar arcæ, cujus amplitudo humanum corpus commode

form of *loculus* has been shewn to be of common occurrence in Judea and in the immediate neighbourhood of Jerusalem. The pains which Arculfus takes to guard against misapprehension are very remarkable, stating that the *loculus* or Sepulchre proper is *not* hollowed to the *exact shape* of the body; that it is *cavern-like in form*, situated on the *north side* of the chamber, but yet having its opening *at its side*, and facing the *south part of the chamber*. All these particulars correspond with the common form above explained. And this explanation is confirmed by other authorities. Thus Paschasius Radbertus, who died A. D. 851, describes the Monument, in his Commentary on St Matthew's Gospel[1], on the authority of many who had

---

capere potest, ut intellexi ab illis qui ipsum viderunt antequam illis tabulis operiretur et quando fuit opertus." p. 510.

Mr Wilde, on the authority of Mr Nicolayson, relates that an old Greek priest told him, that on the morning after the fire of 1808 he went into the tomb, and that as the white marble coating was broken across and not yet replaced, he saw beneath it a plain trough or sarcophagus hewn out of the floor of the church. Wilde's Madeira, &c. Vol. II. p. 295.

Schultz also thinks that a hollow sunk cavity, like a sarcophagus, is under the altar-slab of the present Sepulchre. A cavity of nine inches or less in depth, would satisfy the above descriptions, provided we suppose, which is consistent with the Jewish practice, that the body was not to have been covered with a horizontal lid.

[1] "Monumentum Christi non ita fuit præcisum ut hac in terra monumenta formantur, eo quod ostium habuisse memoratur. Hinc verum esse credimus, quod multi tradiderunt qui eum viderunt, quod domus fuerit rotunda, post ostium monumenti intus, infra rupem vastissimam præcisa, tantæ altitudinis ut intra stans homo vix manu extenta possit ejus culmen attingere, et est illud ostium ab Oriente, cui lapis ille magnus valde advolutus atque oppositus fuit. Non multi siquidem lapides sed unus et ipse magnus....Cujus monumenti, quia cœpimus formam et modum positionis ad intelligentiam narrare visionum, necesse est explicemus. Erat enim, ut dixi, introitus ejus ab Oriente, ac deinde illuc ingredientibus, erat a dextris ille locus in parte Aquilonis, qui specialiter Dominici corporis receptu paratus est; septem quidem pedibus longus, trium vero mensura palmarum reliquo pavimento eminentur. Qui non vulgarium more Sepulchrorum desuper patulus idem factus est locus, sed a latere me-

seen it, nearly in the words of Arculfus, and is careful to explain that the Sepulchre differed from those which were employed in his time. For, in the first place, it had a door, that it was a "round house," and within excavated from a mighty rock, and so on; then, after describing the *loculus*, he adds, "This is not formed after the common manner of Sepulchres, with the opening above, but the opening is entirely along the side, by which the body can be laid therein[2]." The capacity of the chamber was somewhat greater in Arculfus' time than it now is, but perhaps not more than may be accounted for by the space occupied by the artificial lining of the chamber, and the construction of the altar which covers the *loculus*. A space of about three feet wide in front of the altar, at present, as we have shewn, admits three kneeling persons and the attendant priest. And this, with the additional eight inches that would probably be given to each dimension were the lining removed, might have contained the nine men of Arculfus, who prayed in a standing position.

The round form which Arculfus gives to it can only apply to the exterior, although he does not allude to the square shape of the chamber; for it cannot be supposed that its form would have been so completely changed by the artificial lining; and indeed Willibaldus alludes to the square shape.

The difference between its ancient and present state may therefore be summed up as follows. It was originally somewhat more capacious, had no lining of

ridiano, per totum a qua parte Corpus posset imponi." (Mag. Bibl. Vet. Patrum. Col. Agr. 1618. t. 9. n. 2. p. 1229.)

[2] Later writers use exactly the same phrases. Marinus Sanuto, in 1321, has "Qui locus non desuper sed a latere meridiano totus patulus est, unde corpus inferebatur." L. iii. p. 7.

marble, and the receptacle of the body was an arched recess hewn out of the side of the room: whereas, now it is wholly lined with marble, and the so-called receptacle of the body is an altar, within the room, and constructed of marble slabs. I say *within* the room, for the vault or ceiling extends over the altar, as may be seen in the drawings of Le Brun and of Bernardino. It must also be remarked, that Arculfus makes no allusion to the Ante-chapel of the Angel; and it will appear, by comparing his descriptions with some of the succeeding ones, that this Angel Chapel was a subsequent addition.

The event which affected the ancient arrangements of the Sepulchre described by Arculfus, was the demolition of the Church by Hakem[1]; and this was not, like the former destruction by the Persians, part of an indiscriminate and furious attack upon the entire city, by a victorious and barbarian army, but was the deliberate and systematic purpose of a Mahommedan ruler to annihilate the great Christian sanctuary; and his orders were carried out so minutely, that an attempt was even made to eradicate the rock-chamber and its Sepulchre, which are the immediate objects of this chapter. The cotemporary historian Glaber relates that the agents of Hakem "endeavoured to break in pieces even the hollow tomb of the Sepulchre with iron hammers, but without success;" and Ademar states that "when they found it impossible to break in pieces the stone of the monument, they tried to destroy it by the help of fire, but that it remained firm and solid as adamant[2]."

---

[1] See Part I. p. 348, above.

[2] "Ipsum quoque concavum Sepulchri tumulum ferri tuditibus quassare tentantes minime valuerunt." Gla-

Soon after this, the capricious humour of the tyrant was utterly changed, and he ordered the demolished structure to be rebuilt and restored as well as it could be[3]. This was undertaken in the very year of its destruction, A.D. 1010, according to some authors, but William of Tyre places the rebuilding in 1048. We have, however, no accounts of it from the pens of any travellers who visited it, until after Jerusalem fell into the hands of the Crusaders in 1099. They undertook a complete rebuilding and rearrangement of great part of the Church, which will be fully considered below. The changes which were made in the Sepulchral Chapel will appear from the passages of various writers which follow.

Sæwulf describes the whole group of edifices in 1102, evidently before the Crusaders had begun their alterations; and of the portion in question he says, "In the midst of the Church is the Lord's Sepulchre, girt about with a strong wall and covered over, lest rain should fall upon the sacred Sepulchre, for the Church overhead is open to the sky[4]."

But the words of Phocas[5] (A. D. 1185) are, "The cave which was employed for the Sepulchre of the Lord's body is *divided into two parts*, in one of which is deposited the stone which was rolled away from the door; in the other, on the North part, a polished stone

bri Rod. Hist. Bouquet, Tom. x. p. 34. "Lapidem vero monumenti cum nullatenus possent comminuere ignem copiosum superadjiciunt, sed quasi adamas immobilis mansit et solidus." Ex Chron. Ademari. Bouquet, Tom. x. p. 152.

[3] See Part I. p. 351, above.

[4] "In medio autem istius ecclesiæ est Dominicum sepulchrum muro fortissimo circumcinctum et opertum, ne dum pluit pluvia cadere possit super sanctum Sepulchrum, quia ecclesia desuper patet discooperta." Relatio de Peregrinatione Sæwulfi. Tom. IV. Recueil de Voyages. Par. 1839.

[5] Apud Leonis Allatii Σύμμικτα. Lib. I. p. 21.

as long as the apartment is raised a cubit: upon this the Giver of Life was laid....This is ornamented round about with pure gold, the gift of my noble master the Emperor, Manuel Porphyrogenitus Comnenus."

A writer, describing Jerusalem as it existed before it fell into the hands of the Saracens in 1187, proceeds to the Sepulchre. And after stating that round about the monument was the circular Church open above, he adds, "And within this monument was the rock of the Sepulchre, and the monument was covered with a vault at the *chavech* of the monument, and so also above the altar without, which was called *chavec;* and there they chanted always at break of day[1]."

Willibrandus ab Oldenborg in 1211 gives some useful particulars respecting the state of the interior of the Sepulchral chamber, which he says was covered on all sides with white and polished marble, and had within it the very stone upon which the Holy Body was laid; which, entire *and covered with marble,* is open in three places to the touch and kiss of the pilgrims[2]. The

[1] "Et dedans cest le monument estoit la pierre dou sepulcre, et li monumens couvers a voute au chavech de cel monument, ausi com au chief de l'autel par dehors, que l'on apeloit chavec; là chantoit en chascun jour au point du jour." In Beugnot's "Assises de Jérusalem," Tome II. p. 531. *Chavec* (or *chevet*, the apse or round termination of a church,) is here, in the first place, applied to the western end of the Sepulchre, and secondly, to the apse in the Angel Chapel.

[2] In cujus medio, (sc. Ecclesiæ Sancti Sepulchri) quia tota est rotunda, intravimus monumentum Dominicum; quod admodum amplæ et quadratæ cistæ depositum, ex omni latere albo et polito marmore contectum, in se habet ipsam petram, cui illud sacrosanctum corpus Domini, in ara crucis torridum, fuit impositum; quæ etiam, integra et marmore contecta, in tribus locis patet tactui et osculis peregrinorum, de quo Marcus ait, *et posuerunt eum in monumento de petra exciso.* In illo etiam vidimus locum ad dexteram, in quo Angelus apparuit tribus Mariis, et tangit Sanctus Marcus dicens, *Et introeuntes in monumentum, viderunt juvenem a dextris sedentem coopertum stola candida.* Et nota, quia, erga monumentum ipsa ecclesia nec habet nec unquam habuit tectum: ita

latter arrangement is also mentioned by the Russian Abbot, Daniel, who visited Palestine about 1125, and relates that the rocky ledge, a slab (cut out of the same rock as the cave) upon which the Body of our Lord was laid, is now covered with marble, and there are in the front three circular openings, by means of which you may see and kiss the holy stone. He adds, that the outside of the cave is wrought with marble and with *twelve* columns; and that it has a fair upper story upon columns, with a dome covered with cloth of silver, gilded over, and surmounted by a silver image of Christ, rather above the size of life, placed there by the Franks[3].

These descriptions compared with that of Arculfus and others prior to the operations of Hakem, prove that the Sepulchral chamber had now assumed an appearance not very dissimilar from that which it still bears, although it is impossible to say whether the Crusaders were the first so to fit up its interior with a marble lining, and a marble altar-like covering for the *loculus*, or whether they found this already effected

---

ut ipsum tectum ad dispositionem et formam clericalis coronæ sit abrasum; ...sic et prædictum tectum est abrasum, ut inter ipsum monumentum et suum aliquando contectum, nullum medium esse videatur et cœlesti gratia custodiatur." Itin. Willebrandi ab Oldenborg. Ap. Leonis Allat. Σύμμικτα, pars I. p. 147.

[3] Robinson informs us, that this Hegumen Daniel was a Russian abbot, (Ἡγούμενος) who visited Palestine in the beginning of the twelfth century. His journal is one of the earliest documents of the old Slavonic language, and was first printed at St Petersburgh in 1837. (Robinson, Bib. Res. Vol. III. App. p. 6.) I have been favoured with a translated extract from his description of the Sepulchre; but the obscurity of some parts of it make it very difficult to understand his entire meaning. Symeon Symeonis in his Itinerarium, A. D. 1322, relates that the Sepulchre is covered entirely with white marble, so that it can only be seen and touched by means of three small holes in its Southern side. (Itineraria Sym. Symeonis, et Will. de Worcestre. Nasmith, 1778. p. 70.) Rudolph von Suchem confirms this in 1336. (Reyssbuch, p. 845).

by those who had rebuilt the round Church before their arrival. The Angel Chapel, distinctly mentioned and for the first time by Phocas, (A.D. 1185) is not alluded to by Sæwulf, whose rough description of the strong wall and roof that protected the Rock-cave, without mention of columns or decoration, appears to shew, what indeed is most probable from the pointed arches, that the decoration, inside and out, of the cave, was the work of the Crusaders, and that moreover the Angel Chapel[1] was a subsequent contrivance. And although

[1] The plan, fig. 7. and the drawings of Bernardino and others, shew that the Angel Chapel was probably added as an after-thought, to the front of the apse, when the Western part of the Sepulchre was completed. The cornice of this Western part was higher than that of the Angel Chapel, and carried completely across from K to K, (fig. 7.) The position of the columns at this point, compared with that of the apse within, shew that the arcade was continued in front of the apse, so that two additional columns must have stood, one on each side of the apse; and the East front of this chapel, as it then stood, must have had an arcade of one large circular arch over the apse, and one small pointed one on each side. Thus the Sepulchre presented a form similar to that shewn in Fig. 6, with this difference, that instead of the open colonnade of large dimensions, which I have assigned as characteristic of the Constantinian period, the edifice was surmounted by an arcade in close contact with its sides, and supported by the diminutive shafts of mediæval architecture. Thus there were twelve columns and twelve arches, and this explains the description given above from Daniel, 1125. And it was also surmounted by the upper pavilion and its dome.

Instead of the Angel Chapel, it appears to have been protected by a wall of enclosure, as Sæwulf's description implies, and this may serve to interpret the somewhat obscure description which Edrisi gives of this building. His geography was written in the reign, and under the patronage of Roger, King of Sicily, and finished, A.D. 1154. I shall have occasion to refer to this author below, and will now only quote that, "Upon entering the Church, the spectator finds the Holy Sepulchre, a considerable edifice, having *two doors*, and surmounted by a cupola of a very solid construction, very strong, and made with admirable art." He had previously mentioned the great dome overhead, therefore this cupola is the smaller one, which surmounts the upper story of the Sepulchre. Of these two doors, it afterwards appears, that one faces the North and the other the South. It is not improbable, that such doors were placed in the wall of enclosure, for it will appear below, that

the two chroniclers, Glaber and Ademar, assert that the attempts to destroy and uproot the Rock were vain[2], the change of the internal arrangement of the loculus and the disappearance of the low arch above it, so

---

the church itself had two doors, North and South, for the convenience of admitting and dismissing the pilgrims; and as these doors of the Sepulchre are stated by Edrisi to be placed opposite to the doors of the Church, they were probably contrived with reference to the same system, for the purpose of more readily marshalling the pilgrim-crowd. The Angel Chapel, as already stated, is distinctly mentioned by Phocas, the date of whose tract is unfortunately uncertain, but is fixed by his editor, Allatius, about A. D. 1185, that is, two years before the taking of Jerusalem by Saladin.

But every writer describes this little edifice after his own fancy, and hence great obscurity is introduced. For example, Felix Fabri, (A. D. 1483), an exceedingly minute and gossipping describer, takes it into his head to assign three entrances to the Chapel of the Sepulchre, which would have perplexed us exceedingly, if he had not proceeded to explain that by the first he understands the passage between the two low walls, or rather stone seats, which I have described as flanking the entrance to the Angel Chapel (EE, Fig. 7); and he denominates the space between these low walls an *atriolum* to the Chapel. His second door is thus the door of the Angel Chapel, and his third door, the entrance from the latter Chapel to the cave itself. I mention this merely as an example of the fanciful ideas which we have to guard against in investigations of this kind. I subjoin the passage, as the book is rare. A very limited impression has been lately printed by a literary society at Stuttgart.

"Tria quodammodo habet ostia Sanctum Sepulchrum. Primum est in atriolo, mihi spelunca prima, quod atriolum habet murum non altiorem, nisi quod homo intus existens potest super ventrem jacere in muro, et per ecclesiam circumspicere. Unde aliquoties super ipsum murum sedi, et merces negotiatorum in pavimento inferius perspexi. Verum introitus in atriolum non est prope ostium, quia super caput ingredientis nihil est, cum careat superiori limine. Sed inter duos muros se respicientes est ingressus, qui si essent altiores et limen superponeretur ostium fieret. Secundum ostium est de atriolo in primam speluncam monumenti. Et hoc ostium janua clauditur et seris obfirmatur......Tertium ostium est de illa capella vel prima spelunca in secundam speluncam, in qua est Dominicum sepulchrum." (Vol. I. p. 330.)

[2] The Mohammedan rulers, during the Crusaders' siege of Jerusalem, did not believe that the rock had been previously obliterated by Hakem; for they seriously deliberated upon the policy of destroying it utterly at that time, by rooting up the very rock of the Sepulchre, so as to remove for ever the object for which the Christians strived to obtain possession of the City. This was about ninety years after the attempt of Hakem to effect the same thing. See above, Part I. p. 367.

distinctly described by Arculfus, must lead to the conclusion, that if the agents of Hakem did not succeed or persevere in actually levelling the rock, they could scarcely have failed so to have disfigured and damaged it, as to make it necessary, even for the sake of decency, to cover it with marble. The arched recess above the loculus was probably knocked to pieces, or at least so much so as to admit of the vaulted roof above being carried clear over the whole apartment, thus obliterating the recess-form altogether. And by covering the actual stone couch with marble slabs, it became converted into the appearance of an altar, and indeed was from that time employed for mass[1]. Father Fabri, the most minute of all describers, relates that during his vigils in the Church of the Sepulchre in the year 1480, he determined to examine carefully whether any rocky surface remained uncovered in any part of the Sepulchral Chapel or chamber, and for this purpose he took a lighted candle, and curiously scrutinized every part of it within and without. He found the outside wholly covered with marble. Similarly, the door of the Angel Chapel and the walls on each side within presented a marble surface. But he found the wall, which is opposite to the entrance of this Chapel, and in which the little door to the Sepulchre is formed, to be a naked rock, in one piece without joints, and still shewing the marks of tools. In its upper parts, indeed, it was broken, and repaired with stones and cement. Whence he draws the conclusion, that the Holy Sepulchre had been

[1] Another hypothesis may be, that the recessed loculus actually exists, in whole or in part, behind the North side of the present casing, and that the altar now exhibited is vacant, and stands not over, but in front of, the true Sepulchre.

formerly destroyed, but not altogether rooted up, and then had been repaired, and covered with marble to prevent the pilgrims from knocking off little pieces to carry away as relics, and that for the same reason the slab with three openings, already described, was placed in front of the sepulchral couch to hinder the pilgrims from boring holes in it with iron tools, as they were wont to do in order to get off portions. He lays great stress upon this indiscreet zeal of the pilgrims, which he tells us was carried to so great an excess in all ages, that many people think it impossible that they can have left in that place a piece of the true rock so big as a grain of millet[2]. The presence of uncovered rocky surface in the sides of the door is also testified by Mr Wilde, as I have already mentioned, and indirectly

[2] I subjoin the entire original passage, from the Stuttgart Edition, Vol. I. p. 335, 6. "Accepi candelam accensam in Ecclesia Sancti Sepulchri, dum in ea vigilarem, et ad Dominicum monumentum accessi, curiosissime perscrutans, an aliquid non marmore tectum possem videre, et ab extra per circuitum, totum inveni marmore tectum. Ingressus per primum ostium anterioris capellæ parietes utriusque lateris marmore vestitas inveni, sed parietem ante faciem meam, qui dividit speluncam anteriorem ab interiore, in quo est ostiolum ad Dominicum sepulchrum, nudum inveni, et adhibito lumine petræam parietem vidi, non quadris compositam, sed integram, in qua instrumentorum ferreorum signa manifeste apparent. In superiori tamen parte videtur ruptura fuisse, quæ lapide et cæmento est resarcita. Ex quibus videbatur mihi, quod Dominicum sepulchrum fuisset aliquando destructum, sed numquam ex toto erutum, et jam stat reparatum, et sicut hodie stat, ita stetit plus quam ducentos annos, nisi jam est diligentius marmore vestitum, ne peregrini de parietibus lapillos eruant pro reliquiis, et propter eandem causam deposita fuit a Sancto Sepulchro tabula cum tribus foraminibus, de quo supra habetur, quia peregrini foramina cum instrumentis ferreis forabant ad accipiendum aliquid. Quamvis peregrini semper conati fuerint recipere particulas de Sancto Sepulchro, numquam tamen admissum est eis, sed alii lapides porriguntur loco veræ petræ. Semper enim assunt Dominico sepulchro custodes; qui prohibent corrodere volentes. Ideo non valet, quod illi dicunt de indiscreta devotione fidelium, qui, et si habeant illam indiscretam devotionem, tamen non admittitur eis ut indiscrete agant."

by Dr Clarke, who mentions the rugged and broken state of the entrance, but describes it as arising from the pieces knocked off as relics from the marble covering.

It is clear, however, from the words of Fabri, that there was a prevalent opinion in his time that the rock-cave under its marble covering was in a very mutilated condition, which appears to me to be very probable. I suspect that the original rocky roof of the cavern has disappeared. But as the real extent of the damage done, and the state of the rocky nucleus of the present building cannot be ascertained without uncovering it, more words need not be wasted upon this discussion; the only purpose of which has been to shew, that the present improbable Sepulchre is a mere casing of the twelfth century, and that its form, as described by earlier witnesses, was in perfect accordance with the other sepulchral monuments of Judæa.

The inroad of the Charismians, in the thirteenth century, was productive of fresh acts of violence and injury to this Church, and especially to the Sepulchre itself. The letter which was sent by the Patriarch of Jerusalem to Europe, contains the following passage, dated Acon, Nov. 25, 1244.

"With sighs we inform you that sacrilegious hands have inflicted manifold defacements upon the Sepulchre of the Resurrection. The marble pavement that encircled it has been torn up. The mount Calvary, where our Lord was crucified, and the whole Church, has been defiled beyond description. The sculptured columns, which were placed for ornament against the Sepulchre of the Lord, they have carried off, and sent, in token of victory and contempt for the Christians, to the Sepulchre of the wicked Mahomet. And they have violated the tombs of the kings in the said Church, and have scattered their bones[1]."

This curious anecdote may serve to explain the irregular form of the columns shewn in Breydenbach's cut, and mentioned by Bernardino, as they were probably taken from other ruined structures to replace those that were carried off as above related. The rough state in which Baldensel found this monument in 1336, and which excited his disgust, may perhaps have arisen from this or similar assaults which had not then been repaired, or from the gradual state of ruin, which the difficulty of obtaining permission to repair it from the Mohammedan rulers, would necessarily have brought it to.

The last repair, (always excepting the Greek works in 1810), was by Father Bonifacius in the sixteenth century. A letter written by himself is extant, giving an account of this, and it may be found at length in Quaresmius[2]. This Bonifacius, as he himself says, being

---

[1] "Cum suspiriis intimamus, quod in sepulchrum Resurrectionis Dominicæ manus sacrilegas extendentes, illud multipliciter deturparunt. Tabulatum marmoreum quod circumcirca erat positum funditus evertentes, et montem Calvariæ, ubi Christus extitit crucifixus, et totam ecclesiam, ultra quam dici valeat, in omni turpitudine quantum in se fuerat, fœdaverunt. Columnas vero sculptas, quæ ante sepulchrum Domini erant ad decorem positæ, sustulerunt: illas in Christianorum contumeliam ad sepulcrum sceleratissimi Machometi in signum victoriæ transmittentes, et violatis sepulchris felicium Regum in eadem ecclesia collocatis, eorum ossa in Christianorum injuriam disperserunt." Letter from the Patriarch of Jerusalem, &c. to Europe, describing the inroad of the Charizmians, dated Acon, Nov. 25, 1244. Matt. Paris, p. 557. Wats.

[2] "Pater Bonifacius Stephanius, Dei dono et Apostolicæ sedis gratia Stagni Raccusini Episcopus, universis has litteras inspecturis salutem in Domino sempiternam. Cum anno salutis nostræ MDLV. fabrica illa celeberrima ab Helena Sancta, Magni Constantini matre, jam olim structa S.D.N.R. Sepulchrum in orbem claudens, non sine Christianæ pietatis injuria, ruinam minaretur, ac jam fermè collapsa esset, fe. re. Julius Papa tertius (quem ad hanc rem perficiendam æterni nominis ac perpetuæ memoriæ invictissimus

in the year 1555 Prefect of the Convent of St Francis at Jerusalem, it happened that "that celebrated fabric, formerly constructed by St Helena, which encloses the Sepulchre of the Redeemer, was then threatening ruin, and, in fact, was nearly falling," whereupon Pope Julius III., at the request of the Emperor Charles V. and of his son Philip, commissioned him to repair the sacred place; the Emperor having assigned for the purpose a considerable sum of money, and the permission of the Turkish Sultan having also been obtained at great expense, and after much negotiation. "It plainly appeared necessary that the structure should be taken down to the very ground, in order to make an effectual and enduring restoration. And when it was destroyed, the Sepulchre of the Lord, cut in the rock, appeared openly before our eyes: on which two Angels were seen painted above, of which one was saying (in an inscription), *He is*

Carolus quintus Romanorum Imperator, nec non Deo gratus Philippus ejus filius inclytus precibus pulsarunt) instantem ruinam dolens, nobis, qui id temporis Conventus Sancti Francisci de Observantia Ierosolymis Præfectum Apostolica auctoritate agebamus, obnixè præcepit, ut sacrum collabentem locum quamprimùm refici instaurarique curaremus.........Cùm igitur ea structura solo æquanda necessario videretur, ut, quæ instauranda denuò moles erat, firmior surgeret, diuturniorque permaneret, ea diruta, sanctissimi Domini Sepulchrum in petra excisum nostris sese oculis apertè videndum obtulit: in quo Angeli duo depicti superpositi cernebantur; quorum alter scripto dicebat: *Surrexit, non est hic;* alter verò Sepulchrum digito notans, *Ecce locus ubi posuerunt eum.* Quorum imagines, ubi primùm vim aëris senserunt, magna ex parte dissolutæ sunt. Cùm verò lamina una alabastri ex iis, quibus Sepulchrum operiebatur, et quas Helena sancta ibi locaverat, ut super iis sacrosanctum Missæ mysterium celebraretur, necessitate urgente, commovenda esset, apparuit nobis apertus locus ille ineffabilis, in quo triduo Filius hominis requievit; ut planè cœlos apertos videre tunc nobis, et illis, qui nobiscum aderant, omnibus videremur, &c. &c. &c. Datum Stagni in ædibus nostris, sub die 13 Maii, anno à Christo nato supra septuagesimum millesimo quingentesimo." (Quaresmius, Tom. II. p. 512. He copies it from Gretser's "Apologia pro sancta Cruce." Op. Gretseri, 1734, Tom. I. p. 64.)

risen, He is not here, and the other, pointing with his finger to the Sepulchre, above the inscription, *Behold the place where they laid Him!* But when these figures were exposed to the air for a little while, they faded away almost entirely. It was found absolutely necessary to remove one of the alabaster slabs with which the Sepulchre was covered, and which Saint Helena had placed there to enable the mystery of the Mass to be celebrated. And when this was taken away, there appeared open to us all who were present, that ineffable place in which the Son of Man rested for three days."

He goes on to relate that he found therein a piece of wood carefully wrapped in a *sudarium,* which latter, however, fell to dust as soon as it was exposed to the air: this wood, he supposes to have been a piece of the true Cross, and he placed a part of this in the Chapel of the Apparition near the Sepulchre, where it was long preserved. It is very clear that the fabric which was the subject of this repair, was not the great Rotunda, but merely the little chapel which encloses the Rock-tomb, or rather as much as remains of it; and it is evident that the works, which he attributes to S. Helena, are simply those of the Crusaders. It is not so easy to determine how much, after all, was done to this little building upon this occasion. If it was wholly taken down and rebuilt, its original form was exactly preserved, for a rude wood-cut given by Breydenbach in his travels (A. D. 1502), corresponds exactly with the drawings of Zuallardo, Bernardino, and Le Brun, making due allowance for the style of execution; and this cut represents even the wooden chapel which the Copts had set up against the western end of the structure. Probably the part that was entirely taken down and reconstructed was the Angel Chapel, which has been shewn to be an artificial structure, without a rocky nucleus; and also the marble lining of the rock-sepulchre must have been reset. The slab with three openings in front of the tomb is not mentioned after the time of Bonifacius, and seems then to have been replaced by an unpierced one, as at present.

But it is a curious fact, that Father Bonifacius, when describing the rock sepulchres that still exist in the neighbourhood of Jerusalem, relates, that among them he found one in all respects similar to the Holy Sepulchre, which he shewed to his Franciscan brethren, that they might rejoice therein, and exhibit it to their successors and the pilgrims; "and I must know the truth of this resemblance," adds he, "because I saw the very spot where the Holy Body was laid, when I restored that sacred place from its very foundations, and decorated it with the most brilliant marbles, under Paulus IV. and Charles V., &c.[1]" This cave, he says, was amongst a number, which were termed the Retreat of the Apostles; and Zuallardo describes certain cave-sepulchres on the Mount of Offence, opposite to Sion, on the north side of Jerusalem, one of which he asserts to be that which Bonifacius had pointed out; and he has given a sketch of it, from which and from his description it appears that the loculus or receptacle of the body is not in the form of a chest or modern tomb, but is a cavity cut out of the side of the chamber, extending from one end

[1] P. Bonifacius, De perenni cultu Terræ Sanctæ lib. 2. as quoted by Quaresmius, p. 283. The book itself is very scarce, and I have not been able to obtain a sight of it. Robinson was equally unsuccessful. (Bib. Res. Vol. III. App. p. 13.)

Pope Julius III. reigned from 1550, and Paul IV., from 1556. Philip II. succeeded his father Charles V. in 1556, and 1556 is the year when the repairs began.

to the other, its bottom being flat and raised about two feet above the floor, and its upper surface or soffit also flat and parallel to the lower one, with just space enough between them for the body to be pushed into its place. In fact, it precisely resembles the form of the ordinary receptacles for bodies, which are to be seen in the Christian catacombs of Rome. This, if the upper surface were curved into the form of an arch, would correspond exactly with the descriptions of Arculfus and other early writers, which, as I have already shewn, certainly represent the sepulchral cavity as a cavern-like opening excavated out of the rocky wall of the chamber, and not as an altar-tomb, *standing within it*, as the present structure is arranged[2].

[2] Cotovicus (p. 181) completely adopts this view, and even borrows Zuallardo's cut of the said Hill Tomb to represent the Holy Sepulchre, adding, that it is evident that it was not after the fashion of a square tomb open at top, as many think, and as it is always represented; but was cut in the north side of the cave, and open to the south, where the body was inserted so that those who looked in through the small door of the cave, might easily see the place where the body had lain, and also the linen clothes and the napkin, all which they could not have done if it had been a hollow tomb. In describing the rock tombs of Macri, the ancient Telmessus, Clarke says, (Vol. II. p. 252), "A small rectangular opening, scarcely large enough to pass through, admitted us to the interior—where we found a square chamber with one or more receptacles for dead bodies, shaped like baths, upon the sides of the apartment, and neatly chiselled in the body of the rock:" and afterwards (p. 549), relates that on the sides of the Hill of Offence, facing Mount Sion, he found a number of excavations in the rock, similar to those of Telmessus (described in the above passage), each chamber containing one or many repositories for the dead, like cisterns carved in the rock upon the sides of those chambers. "The sepulchres themselves *are stationed in the midst of gardens.*" "One particularly attracted our notice, from its extraordinary coincidence with all the circumstances attaching to the history of our Saviour's tomb: the large stone that once closed its mouth, had been, perhaps for ages, rolled away. Stooping down to look into it, we observed within, a fair sepulchre, containing a repository upon one side only, for a single body, whereas in most of the others there were two, and in many of them more than two." (p. 555). The tomb which Bonifacius indicated as the likeness of the Holy Sepulchre, as

Before I quit the subject of Rock-tombs, I must describe another, which still remains in the neighbourhood of the Holy Sepulchre, and which affords important collateral evidence for its genuineness. This rock-tomb (or rather as much of it as remains), is now included within the Church (see Plan, Fig. 4, No. 6). At the extreme west end of the Rotunda, in the wall of the side-aisle, there is an apse, and from the south side of this apse a low door opens to a small apartment, so low that there is scarcely room to stand upright, and which may perhaps hold three men at once; the eastern side of it is the wall of the Rotunda[1], but the other sides are hewn out of the natural rock, and in this rock sepulchral cavities are excavated horizontally in the sides. On the floor also are the openings of graves sunk downwards in the earth. These tombs have been attributed to Nicodemus and to Joseph of Arimathæa. Some later writers suggest them to have belonged to the time of the Crusaders. But Schultz, from whose "Jerusalem" I have transcribed the description of this cavern, sagaciously remarks, that although the graves on the floor may probably be due to the Crusaders, the sepulchres in the face of the rock are so precisely like those which are to be seen throughout the Necropolis in the environs of Jerusalem, that there can be no doubt that they are the remains of a rock-tomb, formed long before the Church was built, and probably belonged to an old Jewish sepulchre of an age prior to the destruction of Jerusalem by the Romans.

---

he had seen it during the repair, was amongst this very group, and perhaps the identical one that Clarke selected from observation alone, as the sacred cave itself.

[1] A view of this tomb is given by Lord Nugent, Lands Classical and Sacred, Vol. II. p. 34.

The rocky sides of this chamber are not exactly in the direction of the cardinal points, and it appears to be a portion of a rock-chamber, of which the Eastern parts have been cut away, and intruded upon by the process of hewing away the face of the rocky cliff in the brow of which it was originally excavated. For, as the section of the Church shews (Plate 3), the rock rises high against the external wall at the West, and the present level of the floor has been obtained by sinking into the rock. Thus an important corroboration is afforded of the history of the present disposition of the Holy Sepulchre. For instead of supposing the cavern to have been originally formed in a little hillock of rock, as some imagine, the very nature of the ground at present shews that the rock, which now rises behind the Western wall of the Church, was once extended so much farther Eastward as to bring the natural brow of its cliff to the front of the Holy Sepulchre, which was thus naturally formed in the face of this cliff in the usual manner. The Sepulchre just described under the name of Joseph of Arimathæa, was possibly part of a catacomb with many apartments and vestibules like that of the Judges, and at all events its entrance was formed in the face of the cliff, South-west of the entrance of the Holy Sepulchre[2].

[2] I have already stated, that throughout this dissertation I have applied the term Holy Sepulchre to that which is exhibited under this name in the church, without intending to assume its identity with the Sepulchre of the Gospel narrative, which must principally be determined by topographical considerations. To shew that the arrangements of this Sepulchre are not inconsistent with Sacred history, may afford some slight arguments in its favour, but it could hardly be supposed that those who first asserted this cave to be the genuine one, would have selected one which was at variance with the gospel account. From the sacred narrative, however, we gather that the true Sepulchre was an apartment hewn out of the rock, and not a mere grave in the rock;

But as this question of the original form of the ground can hardly be made intelligible until the whole

---

for the disciples are described as "entering into it," in a manner that shews the entrance to have been perfectly easy, when they were not hindered from going in by feelings of awe and reverence. But those who were so hindered were compelled to stoop, (John xx. 5, 11) in order to look in, whence we may either infer that the door was low, or that the stooping posture was necessary to allow the light to enter; but not that the cave was at a lower level than the entrance, for then the disciples would have been said to have "gone down into" the Sepulchre, instead of simply "entering it," which is the phrase always used. The vision of angels "sitting, the one at the head and the other at the feet where the body of Jesus had lain," (John xx. 12) is sufficient to shew that the Sepulchre was of that form in which the body was laid parallel to the side of the apartment. Also it was, more probably, deposited upon a stone couch, than in a hollow *soros*, or sarcophagus. For as the linen clothes appear to have been folded and laid in the place where the body had been, they could hardly have been seen by the disciple, who merely stooped down and looked in at the door, (John xx. 5) if they had been placed at the bottom of a stone chest, but would easily have been seen, if lying upon a stone couch. The vision of angels sitting may be thought to contradict the arched recess above the stone couch; at all events this recess could not have been very low, but in many of these rock tombs it is sufficiently high to allow space for persons to sit, as for example, in the arches represented in the Tombs of the Judges. Plate 4.

There is no allusion in the scripture to a vestibule or outer cave, but on the other hand there is nothing to contradict its existence, and the common arrangement of the Jewish sepulchres makes it probable that there was one.

The cave in the Sakhrah under the dome of the Mosk of Omar, which Mr Fergusson supposes to have been the true Sepulchre, has no resemblance to any sepulchral chamber, either in Jerusalem or elsewhere. It is in form an irregular trapezium, the average height seven feet and superficial area about 600 feet. In the centre of the rocky pavement is a circular slab of marble which when struck returns a hollow sound, clearly indicating a well or excavation beneath, (Bartlett's Walks, p. 154) and there is a corresponding opening in its rocky roof. It is wholly below the surface, and the access to it by a flight of steps; there is no provision for the reception of a body either in the form of recess, or stone couch, or any other of the wonted indications of sepulchral purpose which characterise such chambers. But, on the contrary, the aperture in the roof corresponding to the other in the floor shew a purpose which it would be difficult to connect with a sepulchre, but which I shall endeavour to explain in the Essay on the Temple.

It does not seem to have occurred to Mr Fergusson that sepulchral caverns have characteristic arrangements and forms that mark their destination, and

Church, and especially Mount Calvary, has been described, I will reserve its fuller explanation for a separate section, and will now proceed to describe the group of buildings that surround the Sepulchre.

VIII.

THE CHURCH OF THE HOLY SEPULCHRE.

I HAVE in the preceding sections entered at great length into the history and description of the Chapel of

---

that therefore it is not enough to produce a mere hole in a rock, like that of the Sakhrah, which is not only deficient in any of the usual indications of such a purpose, but is even contradictory in many particulars to the examples of rock sepulchres with which it is surrounded.

Moreover, Mr Fergusson (Jerusalem, p. 88) asserts that the Evangelists all agree that those that came to look for the body of Christ, "looked down into the Sepulchre," and he marks these latter words as if he were quoting the exact words of holy writ, which I need hardly say is not the case. To "stoop down," in order to look into an apartment is not necessarily to "look down into." Again, he says with equal recklessness, that in the modern building the tomb is several feet above the pavement of the Church, and if that pavement and the filling-up were removed they must have stood on tiptoe to have looked in. Bernardino's drawings, which appear to be this gentleman's authority, are partly in section and partly in elevation, and his wood-engraver by converting the outside into modern strict elevation and exaggerating the inside has contrived to raise the floor of the cave about two feet above the pavement of the Church; but Bernardino's figures (32, 33) represent the matter very differently. If the fact were so, it has no bearing upon the question, for the rough rock about the Sepulchre must have been so levelled as to change the relation of the outside to the floor of the chamber, which after all, like most of these sepulchres, was probably about the same level as the sill of the outer door.

Mr Fergusson has thus utterly failed in shewing either the probability of the Sakhrah cave having been intended for a sepulchre, or in demonstrating the absurdity of supposing the so-called Holy Sepulchre to be other than an artificial construction. His opinions concerning the architecture of the Mosk of Omar, which he believes to be the church of Constantine, shall be considered in their proper place.

I will only remark upon the total absurdity of locating a place of common execution and sepulture close under the walls and upon the same platform as the Sacred Temple of the Jews.

the Holy Sepulchre. The buildings that are attached to and partly surround it, will be understood by a comparison of the plans (Plate 2), with the sections (Plate 3) which represent the Church as it appears to have remained from the expulsion of the Crusaders in 1187 to the fire of 1808, which I have termed the fourth period of the buildings. But it will be remembered that the Crusaders found the Rotunda and some other buildings already erected, and that their works consisted of additions to those which already existed, and in some necessary alterations. The works of the Crusaders are therefore distinguished from the earlier ones by a different and lighter tint on the Plan.

The Holy Sepulchre (1, 2, Plate 2)[1] stands in the midst of the Rotunda, which was about seventy-three feet in diameter[2], and the height of its walls about

---

[1] The numbers which are introduced in parentheses in the text, are references to the plan, Plate 2.

[2] The diameter of the central part is at present sixty-seven feet English, and the total interior diameter, measured from the walls of the surrounding aisle, is one hundred and twelve English feet. These are the measurements of Mr Scoles. The interior wall was so damaged by the fire of 1808 that it has been rebuilt, but this rebuilding appears to have consisted in a mere casing of the interior surface, retaining the old vaults and triforium around; hence the present diameter is less than the original one. But the diameter of the side-aisle was unaffected by the fire. Bernardino assigns 156 palms to this diameter (p. 33), and declares (p. 1) that he employs the "canna ordinaria" which is used in the kingdom of Naples. If 156 palms are equal to 112 English feet, it follows that his palm is equal to .718 English feet. The nearest value to this in the ordinary tables is the Roman canna d'architettura = .733 English feet, which appears to have been the measure employed by him. The difference is easily accounted for by the inaccuracy in the length of his measuring-rod. The scale which is engraved on his plate is wholly at variance with the measures stated in his text, and is clearly an engraver's blunder; but if a new scale be drawn, by dividing the diameter of the round church upon his plan into 100 palms, it will be found to correspond with all his measures. The diameter of the central rotunda is stated to be one hundred palms by Bernardino, that is, seventy-three English feet. The diameter of the present one is only sixty-seven. If

sixty-eight, so that probably the height and diameter were intended to be equal. The walls are divided in the usual manner into three stories, ground-floor, triforium, and clerestory.

The number of piers on the ground-plan are eighteen, some of which are round pillars with capitals, bases, and pedestals, and the others simple square piers. These two different forms are disposed of as follows. On the North, the West, and the South, respectively, are placed a pair of square piers upon which rests an arch of a rather wider span than those that are interposed between them, and which are sustained by the pillars. The East is distinguished by a pair of larger and loftier piers of a more complex character, sustaining a wider arch (4) that rises into the triforium of the Church, and now serves as an arch of passage between the Rotunda and the Choir; which latter part was erected by the Cru-

we reduce Bernardino's measures to English, we find that the lower pillars stood on pedestals five feet high; and the pillars, including base and capital, were seventeen feet high. The entire height from the pavement to the floor of the triforium was thirty feet, and as the whole height of every upper story was three-quarters of the one below it, the triforium-space was twenty-two feet, and the clerestory-space sixteen feet; the total height from the pavement to the top of the wall was therefore about sixty-eight feet. The precept for making a superior order of columns one-quarter less in proportion than the inferior order, is borrowed from Vitruvius (l. 5. c. 1, and c. 7). Whence we may infer that the good father Bernardino only actually measured the lower story, which he gives in detail, and that he guessed at the height of the others by assuming them to have been erected upon a Vitruvian principle; a very common assumption with the architectural writers of his age.

"I pilastri dunque della cupola maggiore sono alti da terra palmi sei e tre oncie. Le base due, le colonne sedici, e otto oncie, li capitelli quattro, e dieci oncie, e dalla superficie de capitelli insino alla cornice sono palmi nove, e tre oncie, la cornice è palmi due, talche in tutto son palmi quarant' uno, e de gl' altri ordini la quarta meno à proportione......la cupola é alta palmi cinquanta......e in tutto sono di altezza palmi cento quaranta quattro." p. 36.

saders, whereas the Rotunda is the work of the Greek Emperor Monomachus, and was in existence before they obtained possession of Jerusalem. The large arch in question, in the original building, probably opened into a short-chancel terminated by an apse, which apse the Crusaders removed, and erected their piers against the chancel-walls, in the manner shewn by the Plan, and which will be explained more fully below.

The western face of this arch which fronted the Holy Sepulchre, appears to have been more highly ornamented with columns than the rest of the Rotunda. Unfortunately, the only view of the decoration of the arch is that given in the Travels of Zuallardo[1], which is evidently very inaccurate; but it may be concluded that the piers of the arch were ornamented with tiers of columns in a manner somewhat analogous to the lower part of the West front of St Mark in Venice[2], a Church erected in the Eastern style like that of our Rotunda, which resembles it also in the alternate disposition of single arches on plain piers, and of groups of arches on pillars having bases and capitals. The Plan and Elevation will shew the order in which these pillars and arches are set between the piers. The pillars are represented in Le Brun's engraving with regular pedestals and Corinthian capitals; but from the usual inaccuracy with which the artists of his time repre-

[1] This view appears in the Travels of Furer, A.D. 1565. It has been suggested to me that this and other similar engravings of the holy places were made for sale to the pilgrims, and thence copied into books of Travels.

[2] S. Mark was founded A.D. 977 or in 1043, and was finished in 1071, excepting the upper part of the West front. The rotunda of the Sepulchre was begun soon after 1010, and carried on to its completion about thirty years after.

sented mediæval buildings, we may infer that this only means that they had foliated capitals and pedestals of some kind or other[3].

The number of arches in the triforium are exactly equal to that of the pier-arches below, each over each, but the alternation of square piers and round pillars follows a different law. A plain arch, on piers, stands over each similar plain arch below, at the cardinal points, west, north, and south. Between these, however, the arches are disposed in pairs, with a pillar and pier alternately, as shewn in Plate 3, so as to make up, on the whole, ten square piers and eight round pillars[4]. Above the triforium is a clerestory-wall, in which are sunk arched panels, one over each of the arches below. These panels were ornamented with figures in mosaic, on a gilt ground[5], having their names inscribed over their heads, and holding tablets in their left hands, on which certain sentences were written, which may be found in Quaresmius. On the east and west sides, in this writer's time, the figures had all fallen to pieces; but on the south, towards the west, there remained the story of Tobias and the fish; and thence followed in order the Prophets Ezechiel,

---

[3] Pedestals sometimes occur in Greek churches, as in St Sophia and the church at Mistra. See Couchaud, Eglises Byzantines de la Grèce.

[4] The ten piers are exclusive of the piers of the eastern arch. This arrangement of piers and pillars is described in the Italian original text of Zuallardo, who states that the church has "due chiostri, ò anditi, l' uno sopra l' altro; hora di due colonne quadre et un pilastro in mezzo, et hora di due otre, et una colonna." p. 188, ed. Rom. 1587. But the sense is quite perverted in the French translations of this author.

[5] "Fatte di lavoro mosaico indorato," Zuallardo, p. 190. In Canina's great work, Dei Templi Christiani, a restored view of this church is attempted, but evidently very hastily and rashly executed. Amongst other unwarrantable features he has inserted windows instead of the mosaic panels of the Rotunda.

Daniel, and Hosea; the Emperor Constantine, in a niche, in imperial robes, bearing in his right hand a cross and in his left a globe marked with a cross; the Prophets Joel, Amos, and Obadiah. On the north side were the shattered remains of some effigies of the Apostles, with their names, as SS. Thomas, James, Philip, Matthew, Bartholomew, and Simon; and in a niche in the middle, opposite to the Emperor Constantine, was the Empress Helena, similarly robed in a royal dress, bearing the cross and the globe, and having an Angel above. The names of the Emperor and Empress were repeated in Latin and in Greek. Those of the other figures and their accompanying sentences were in Latin only[1].

The roof of the Rotunda was of wood, built of 131 squared cedars, in the form of a single cone truncated at the top, where the light was admitted through a circular aperture, twelve feet, or perhaps more, in diameter. And this was the only opening through which light entered into this part of the Church; but the example of the Pantheon at Rome shews that such a mode of admitting light from a single aperture at the crown of a dome, is amply sufficient. The woodwork of the roof had been ornamented with gilding and silvering. The top of the roof, or margin of the aperture, was 106 feet above the pavement. The ravages of the unhappy fire of 1808 were especially destructive to the Rotunda, for its wooden roof fell a prey to the flames, and excited their fury to such an extent, by

---

[1] I copy this description from Quaresmius, (p. 368) who describes the decorations of the whole church, as far as they remained, very minutely; other travellers merely allude to them; but his residence at Jerusalem enabled him to collect these particulars at leisure.

enabling them to calcine and split the stone-work and marble columns, that it became necessary wholly to rebuild the inner wall which we have been considering. Probably this rebuilding is a mere casing of the old nucleus; and an experienced observer may yet find in the aisles and triforium traces enough to discover the exact dimensions of the parts I have been describing; for the diameter of the new Rotunda is about six feet less than that of the old one. The design is unfortunately wholly different, and of a most heavy and barbarous character, as may partly be seen in the vignette at the beginning of this volume, which shews the wall of the Rotunda in the back-ground. This heaviness may be due to the fact of its being a casing of the old work.

A vaulted side-aisle encircles the Rotunda, but is cut off eastward by a straight wall that extends north and south from the piers of the great eastern arch in the manner shewn by the Plan. The aisle is concentric to the Rotunda for rather more than a semicircle westward, and this portion of the aisle is bounded by a thick wall containing three small apses (5, 7, 8) about twenty-three feet in diameter, of which the northern and southern are not placed exactly upon the diametral line, but so that the whole apse lies to the west of that line. This wall appears to have remained from a very early period, as it naturally would do, and may be supposed to have belonged to the church of Modestus, if not even to the original Basilica of Constantine. The three apses are expressly mentioned by Arculfus (A. D. 697) as also containing altars, but when the altars were removed or abandoned does not appear. The southern apse (5) was in the last century assigned to the Abyssinians, and is now, together with the adjoining aisle, in possession of the Armenians.

The western apse (7), with the adjacent tomb of Joseph of Arimathæa (6) already described, is in the hands of the Syrians. The northern apse (8) has a door opened in its wall, and serves as a passage to the offices outside the Church, as well as to a cistern (10), termed the well of St Helena, which furnishes an abundant supply of water without any apparent spring or well, as Quaresmius relates[1]. Near this door stands (or did stand before 1808) a marble font (9), square on the outside, but cut into the form of a rose within, the *baptisterium* of the old Church, in the words of Quaresmius[2]. In the triforium at the extreme west point was the original west door of the Church, by which it was entered from the contiguous street, before the Mohammedans obtained possession of the city. When they converted this Church into a source of revenue, by taxing the pilgrims, they carefully walled up every entrance to it excepting one door (56) in the south transept, to enable them more conveniently to collect the tax and prevent any person from evading it. The level of this western street is so much higher than the floor of the Rotunda, that it was found more convenient to make the entrance into the triforium at once, than to descend to the lower level by steps from the street. The arch of this doorway may still be seen in Patriarch-street; and is marked in the plan of Jerusalem which accompanies this work. A sketch of it by Mr Arundale, which is lying before me, shews the southern

---

[1] "Nullus est fons vel puteus." Quar. 371.

[2] "Præ foribus ostii est marmoreum vas quadrum, formam rosæ intus præ se ferens." Quar. 371. It is marked in Bernardino's Plan (24) as the Greek font.

half of the hood or porch supported partly on corbels and partly on a column, the lower part of which is enveloped in masonry; and the northern half of this porch is also walled up and concealed by a bridge which crosses the street at this point, connecting the two halves of the Greek convent. My section in Plate 3 exhibits its probable original arrangement.

This doorway is mentioned by Quaresmius (p. 370), and also by Edrisi, in whose time it was in use, and as he says, "The Church is lower than this door, and there is no descent to the lower part from this side; but on the north side is a door which is called the door of St Mary, leading to a staircase of thirty steps[3]." The exact position of the staircase I have not been able to discover; but it was plainly required for the purpose of affording access from below to the triforium, as well as to enable persons who came in at the upper west door from the street, to descend and enter the church at the door below.

The side aisle of the Rotunda has been already described as being concentric only in its western half; for the portions of this aisle immediately in contact with the straight wall which bounds the whole to the east, are of a square form, evidently contrived with respect to the

[3] From the French translation of Edrisi by Jaubert, Paris, 1836. A north triforium door and staircase are mentioned by Bernardino, p. 36. Part of the triforium on the north was in later times fitted up for the use of the Latins, with four apartments, one of which contained an altar of St Didacus; behind which were two rooms, one for the accommodation of pilgrims, and another which served as a sacristy in which they kept their tapestry, lamps, and other matters of value for the service of the church. These particulars appear from the account of the fire in 1808. (See W. Turner's Journal of a Tour in the Levant, 1820. Vol. II. p. 597.) The southern part was, and still is, enclosed to serve as the great church of the Armenians; and here the fire of 1808 began. There is a staircase (67) in the south-east corner of the aisle of the Rotunda, which leads to this Armenian church.

chapels, which are erected both on the north and south extremities of the aisle. On the north wall a door (16) opens to a single chapel, but from the south wall projects a range of three chapels (65, 62, 61), the access to which from the Church is now blocked up, but it was formerly maintained by a door (66) in the south wall of the aisle, exactly opposite to that in the north wall (16) which still leads to the north chapel.

This north Chapel is termed the *Chapel of the Virgin Mary of the Apparition*[1], because the tradition of the place is, that on this spot our Saviour appeared to his mother after the Resurrection. The floor is three or four steps higher than the pavement of the Rotunda, and it has a recess to the east which was furnished with an apse, previously to the late repairs, as shewn in my Plan, but is now square, and in this recess is placed the Altar, which is dedicated to the Virgin Mary, and serves as the High Altar of the Latins in this Church; for the Greeks have possession of the real High Altar in the Choir of the Crusaders. The apse was semicircular within, but polygonal without, in the usual form of the Greek apses; and in fact this Chapel is mentioned by Sæwulf in 1102; and being therefore in existence before the Crusaders began their buildings, was evidently the work of Greek architects.

On each side of the above-mentioned Altar is placed a subordinate Altar, with a recess or niche in the wall above it[2]. The niche over the northern side altar is

---

[1] Sacellum Sanctæ Mariæ Virginis de Apparitione (Quaresmius, p. 568). It is a quadrangular apartment, twenty-one feet four inches broad, and twenty-eight feet long, according to Mr Scoles, exclusive of the altar recess, which is nine feet broad, and seven feet deep.

[2] These recesses are about three feet high, and two wide. (Bernardino, 31.) The side altars also recal Greek ar-

said once to have contained a piece of the true cross[3]. The niche above the southern side-altar contains a portion of a column, nine inches in diameter, and about three feet high[4], of fine porphyry, which goes by the name of the *Column of the Flagellation*, professing to be a piece of the column to which our Saviour was bound and scourged by the order of Pilate[5].

---

rangements, and were probably the usual side-tables of the Eastern ritual. In the middle of the chapel there is a round grey marble slab of three feet diameter, inserted in the pavement, to mark the traditional spot where the three crosses were laid after their discovery by St Helena, and where the miracle was wrought by which the true Cross was distinguished from the others. (Quaresmius, p. 383.)

[3] Quaresmius relates that this piece of the true Cross was left there by the Emperor Heraclius, when he brought back that relic from Persia, in the year 628, upon which occasion it was divided into pieces, and variously distributed, one of them being left at Jerusalem. But this piece was lost at the battle of Tiberias; and when Father Bonifacius found, as already related, a relic in the Sepulchre during its repair in 1555, which he fancied to be a piece of the true Cross, he deposited it in this niche, whence, as they say, it was stolen by the Armenians. At all events, it is not there now. (Quaresmius, pp. 383, 514.) The existence of the chapel is not mentioned before 1102; and the above-mentioned traditions concerning the deposit of the Cross here by Heraclius, the place where Helena caused the three crosses to be laid after they were dug up, &c.; are manifestly of subsequent invention, as well as the tale which Fabri tells, that this chapel stands on the site of a house in which the Virgin took refuge after the Crucifixion. (Vol. I. p. 286.)

[4] Alta palmi tre e mezo, e di diametro un palmo. (Bern. p. 31).

[5] A column, which was part of the structure of the Church at Mount Sion, is mentioned with the legend in question by St Jerome, by the Bordeaux Pilgrim, Arculfus, and others. It was broken by the Mohammedans, but the pieces are said to have been carefully collected about the year 1556, presented respectively to Pope Paul IV., Ferdinand the Emperor, Philip II. of Spain, and to the Venetian Republic, &c. &c. One fragment, however, was at the same time reserved at Jerusalem, and located in the niche where it is now to be seen. A rival column of flagellation is preserved at Rome, in the church of S. Praxede; but I must refer my readers to Quaresmius for a discussion of their respective claims to authenticity. Sæwulf, in 1120, immediately after the Crusaders' conquest, mentions a column of flagellation which was then placed between the *Carcer Christi* and the place of the Invention of the Cross.

The whole chapel of the Apparition is the chapel of the Latin convent of the Franciscan Friars, and is fitted up with seats as a choir for them. Their dwellings are immediately in contact with the northern and western sides of it, as the Plan shews. They took possession of this locality in 1257[1], but were not fully established until 1342, when permission for their residence was obtained of the Sultan, at the intercession of Robert, king of Sicily, and his queen. The Greeks had previously established themselves in the large church, of which they have retained their hold to the present time[2].

But to return to the square vestibule of this chapel. On its East side was a small chapel of St Mary Magdalen, fitted up in what appears to have been originally a doorway (17), and has in the late repairs been made to return to that purpose. Next to this follows an arch (18), which opens to a long corridor (21) running Eastward and in contact with the North transept of the great Church, but evidently belonging to an earlier period, for it has pillars and arches on its Southern side, the spacing and arrangement of which are totally at variance with those of the greater building with which it is in contact. This appears at once by the plan, and there can be little doubt that this is the remains of a cloister which bounded the open area upon

---

[1] Quaresmius, Lib. I. p. 176.

[2] Willibrandus ab Oldenburg, in 1211, found the Church with the Holy Sepulchre, and all that it contained, under the charge of four Syrian priests, who were not allowed to leave the walls, but were left unmolested by the Saracens, (p. 148, Leonis All. Opusc.) In fact, the whole City was under the rule of the Eastern Church, until the Latins wrested it from them at the time of the Crusaders' conquest, and when the latter were driven out, the Easterns resumed possession of the Holy places.

which the Crusaders' choir and central cupola was afterwards erected. This cloister leads to a small, low, dark apartment (23), wherein our Saviour is reported to have been confined during the preparations for the crucifixion, whence it is called the Prison of Christ. The earliest writer that notices this prison is Sæwulf (A.D. 1102), who, enumerating the Holy Places which are to be seen in the atrium of the Church, mentions the "prison where our Lord was confined, according to the Syrian tradition;" and the next is Epiphanius, a Syrian monk, whose description of the Holy Land is of uncertain date, but apparently about the end of the twelfth century. This prison however is not alluded to by any other authors of this period. In the sixteenth century and afterwards it becomes one of the ordinary *stations*. It is needless to add that there is not the slightest ground in Scripture, or even in probability, for supposing that such a prison was employed.

It is of an irregular form, nineteen feet long, and in width sixteen feet at the West end, and eighteen at the East. It is only eight feet in height[3], is three steps below the level of the corridor[4], has no window, and is described as being excavated in the rock:—I presume only the lower part of it, which, as Zuallardo tells us, seems to have been intended for a reservoir of water. Its roof is supported by two rude pillars which divide it into three aisles as it were, and an altar is fixed against its eastern wall.

The southern chapels, (65, 62, 61), which stand directly opposite to the Chapel of the Apparition, are in

---

[3] La volta è alta da terra palmi undici. (Bern°. 31.)

[4] Cotovicus, p. 161.

number three, and these are placed in a series; they have polygonal Greek apses, and their doors were so arranged that in the original state of this Church, as Sæwulf describes it, a person standing in the last or most southern chapel could see through all the *five* chapels in order from door to door, reckoning in the five the Rotunda, as well as the *three* southern chapels, and the northern Chapel of the Apparition. This account is perfectly consistent with the plan, which shews, supposing the doors to be now open, that a straight view might be obtained in the manner described[1].

The middle of these chapels (62) is named the Church of the Trinity both by Sæwulf and the writer in Beugnot, and both mention the baptismal font which it contains; the latter adding that all the women of the city were married in this Church, and all the children baptized there. Afterwards it became the Chapel of St Mary Magdalene, and is thus mentioned by W. Wey in 1447[2], and by Saligniaco, Breydenbach, Quaresmius, and others. It is now the parish-church of the Greeks, and called the Church of the Ointment-bearers, that is to say, of Mary Magdalene and her companions[3]. In the Pilgrim's Guide it is marked as the "Church of the Resurrection." The font (63) is indicated in the Plan in the latter volume.

The Chapel to the south (61) is termed by Sæwulf the Chapel of St James, as also in the Greek plan in

---

[1] In Plate 2, the eastern front of the chapels which form the west side of the court of the Church, is accurately laid down from Mr Scoles' measurements. The chapels themselves still exist, as do the doors, but I have no other authority for their interior arrangement than a wretchedly-constructed Greek Plan in the Προσκυνητάριον by Chrysanthus.

[2] Itinerarium W[i]. Wey, in the Bodleian. He says it was in possession of the Nestorians.

[3] Mark xvi. 1; Luke xxiii. 56.

the Pilgrim's Guide. It appears to be only parted off from the chapel of St Mary Magdalene, and is therefore not mentioned by many writers. Quaresmius describes the latter chapel as having on each side altars of St Nicolas and St Andrew, and adds, that some have held that St James, the first bishop of Jerusalem, called the brother of our Lord, celebrated mass and was consecrated here[4].

The remaining chapel (65) of this group, which lies between the chapel of St Mary Magdalene and the south wall of the Rotunda, is, in fact, the lower story of the campanile of the church. Sæwulf mentions it as the Chapel of St John, and in connexion with the Chapel of St Mary of the Apparition, which is placed in a similar manner on the north side of the Rotunda. He supplies a key to the arrangements by saying, that even as S. Mary and S. John stood on either side of our Lord during his passion, so are their chapels placed on each side of the church. It is also called the Chapel of St John the Evangelist, and of the Forty Martyrs, in the Pilgrim's Guide[5]. Other writers term it simply the campanile.

This campanile, which seems to be gradually falling to decay, was a noble tower of five stories. Unfortunately, the drawings which are given by Breydenbach, Zuallardo, Bernardino, and Le Brun, differ so absurdly from each other in many respects, that it is scarcely credible that they are intended for the same object[6].

---

[4] Quaresmius, T. II. p. 576.

[5] A tract in Leonis Allatii Opusc. p. 91, by a member of the Greek Church, describes the three chapels of the Atrium as those of the Anastasis, the Forty Martyrs, and St James.

[6] The models in the British Museum appear to offer an exceedingly faithful representation of it. From them, and from Le Brun, I have principally derived the sketch in Plate 3. (Vide Appendix.)

The three lower stories still exist, and have been sketched by Roberts and other modern artists, from whose representation it appears that the arches of the windows are pointed. The lower story has been just described as the Chapel of St John, with a polygonal apse; the next story had on the sides that were free from buildings a single pointed arch, the space of which was occupied by three subordinate arches and a quatrefoil opening over them in the usual Romanesque manner. This arch is shewn in the modern sketches, but is walled up, so that the description of the filling-up is, in fact, conjecturally supplied from Bernardino and Zuallardo; the third story[1] rises clear of the roof, and has two plain pointed windows on each face, which still remain: the eastern face has shafts. The fourth and fifth stories have fallen down, but were standing in 1678, when Le Brun's sketch was made. The fourth had two large arches on each face, each arch being subdivided into two, which rested on a single shaft in the middle, and had a quatrefoil over. The fifth story had each face divided into three arches, of which the side ones were panels only, and the middle was open as a window, and was subdivided by a shaft like the arches of the fourth story. Breydenbach (1483) represents the tower complete with a corbel-table, a parapet rising and falling in steps, and the whole surmounted with a leaden octagon dome, having gables on each face. But whether this is supplied from his fancy, or whether the roof really existed in his time, it is impossible to say. The sketches that succeed Breydenbach's exhibit a gradual degradation. The roof

[1] The third, fourth, and fifth story appear, in Plate 3, rising above the roof. It is difficult to ascertain the exact height, but it could not have been less than 130 feet to the top of the parapet.

has disappeared in Zuallardo's view, 1586; Le Brun's, in 1678, appears to be in the same state; but now the two upper stories have fallen.

There are four buttresses, which project in the east and west direction only, and rise nearly to the top of the fourth story; the general style of the architecture appears similar to that of the churches in Sicily; for example, to the campanile of the church called La Martorana in Palermo[2].

I have now described the Rotunda with its adhering chapels, and with the corridor, which leads to the so-called Prison. All this group existed when the Crusaders entered Jerusalem, erected especially with reference to the great object which originated the whole mass of buildings, namely, the Holy Sepulchre. But three other principal Holy Places were situated in the immediate neighbourhood, besides several subordinate ones. To use the words of the cotemporary chronicler William of Tyre, "Previous to the entry of our Latin people into Jerusalem, the place of our Lord's Passion, called Calvary or Golgotha, and the place where the wood of the Life-giving Cross was discovered, and lastly, the place where the Lord's Body, when taken down from the Cross, was anointed, embalmed, and wrapped in fine linen, were exceedingly small oratories on the outside of the great Church. But after, by the Divine assistance, our people had obtained possession of the city, the aforesaid Church appeared to them too small. Having therefore augmented it with the most solid and lofty work, working in and

---

[2] Engraved by Gally Knight, and by Gailhabaud in his Monuments Anciens et Modernes. See also Couchaud, Eglises Byzantines de la Grèce, for a view of the tower of the Church of the Virgin at Mistra.

connecting the old with the new, they marvellously contrived to include the aforesaid holy places[1]."

Of these places the Calvary or projecting rock, upon which it was believed the Cross was planted, is situated immediately to the east of 47 in the plan, and to the west of it is the place of Anointing (50). The place where the Cross was found by St Helena, is at the eastern extremity of the buildings (33), and on a much lower level, as the section (Plate 3) shews.

These places were brought into the present connected series of buildings in the following manner. Removing the apse, which I have supposed to have closed the short chancel (4) of the Rotunda, the present choir, furnished with its circumscribing aisle and radiating chapels, was erected to the east of it in the form then employed in many parts of western Europe, and with pointed arches. A central cupola was placed upon four piers, so adjusted in position that the south transept should include the place of Anointing, and range properly with the three south chapels, so as to form a court of entrance. Room was also then left on the eastern side to adjust the chapel of Calvary, in connexion with the new transept.

---

[1] "Porrò ante nostrorum Latinorum introitum locus Dominicæ passionis qui dicitur Calvaria sive Golgotha, et ubi etiam vivificæ Crucis lignum repertum fuisse dicitur, et ubi etiam de Cruce depositum Salvatoris Corpus unguentis et aromatibus dicitur delibutum et syndone involutum, sicut mos erat Judæis sepelire, extra prædictæ ambitum erant Ecclesiæ, oratoria valde modica. Sed postquam nostri, opitulante divinâ clementiâ, urbem obtinuerunt in manu forti, visum est eis prædictum nimis angustum ædificium: et ampliata ex opere solidissimo et sublimi admodum Ecclesia priore, intra novum ædificium veteri continuo et inserto, mirabiliter loca comprehenderunt prædicta." W. Tyr. Lib. VIII. c. 3.

King Godfrey also instituted *Canons* with *Prebends*, and gave them habitations about the Church, Lib. IX. c. 9; and caused bells to be cast for the Church. Alb. Aquensis, Lib. VI. c. 40. (p. 285.)

The place of the Invention of the Cross was necessarily excluded from the new church, which however was so connected with the chapel of St Helena as to afford access to it by means of a door (28) and stairs leading from the eastern aisle or "procession path," in a manner that will be fully explained as we proceed, and which indeed is shewn by the different tints of the plan.

The great eastern arch (4) of the Rotunda communicates immediately with the central lantern (43) of the choir. This lantern stands upon four noble piers, the centres of which are distant forty feet from east to west, and forty-three from north to south.

The opposite faces of the piers were distant thirty-one feet ten inches, and their height including base and capital was fifty-two feet; which, being by a singular coincidence the very dimensions of the tower-arches of Winchester and Peterborough, may at once give a correct idea of the magnitude of this church, and shew that its proportions were Romanesque[2]. The form of these piers too was strictly Romanesque, having square pier-edges alternating with shafts in a manner that is sufficiently familiar now to the merest tyro in architecture; but seems sorely to have puzzled the draughtsmen and engravers of old, to judge from the various representations which are given of them. In Bernardino's plan the plinths only are seen. In Zuallardo's plan the

[2] The piers of Winchester tower are fifty-three feet in height, from the floor of the transept, and their opposite faces thirty-two feet asunder, which are also the dimensions of Peterborough. The church of S. Martin at Cologne has piers fifty-five feet high, thirty feet apart. Thirty feet, more or less, is a very common width for large churches, and may probably be derived from the twenty cubit width of Solomon's Temple; a cubit being about eighteen inches.

attached shafts are distinctly shewn, but not very accurately, and they appear in some of Bernardino's elevations, but not in others, evidently not being understood by the engraver. In Le Brun's interior view of the choir they are delineated as well as could be expected for that period, and his text describes them unmistakeably. "By grouped columns I understand great columns composed of several smaller ones attached one to the other; or rather, one great column which seems to have others attached to its outer surface. These are alternately square and round; and some of those in question are so large that they appear made up of ten, and even as many as sixteen, of these smaller ones[1]." The great eastern tower-piers have actually sixteen, if we reckon shafts and square edges, proceeding in order round its circumference[2].

Upon the pointed arches of these four piers was erected a circular tambour-wall or lantern, resting on pendentives, and crowned with a cupola. The wall was ornamented with an arcade, which, as shewn in the section, consisted of sixteen arches decorated with shafts, three to each pier, and forty-eight in all, as Le Brun describes. The arches are circular, at least they so appear in Le Brun's view, (grievously distorted by his bad perspective,) as also in the model in the British Museum. They were alternately pierced for windows, and the outside of the wall had four broad pilasters opposite to the cardinal points respectively, with two of these windows between each.

Breydenbach's view also shews the ruins of a small

[1] Le Brun, p. 289. Ed. 1714.

[2] These piers still exist, as well as the four great pointed arches above them, but the cupola was destroyed by the fire.

arched lantern on the top of the cupola. This cupola was ascended by a spiral external stair formed upon its northern surface, as Le Brun's view shews it. The altitude of the crown of the cupola from the pavement was 156 palms or 114 English feet. The great tower arches were pointed and had three orders of voussoirs as well as all the arches and windows of this part of the Church. This character, which never appears in the arches of Greek mediæval buildings, effectually identifies these portions with the Crusaders, and separates them from the Rotunda and the chapel of Helena, in which the arches are simple.

The eastern tower-arch opens to the presbytery of the cruciform structure, which is terminated by an apse. The seats of the choir are placed under the central lantern. It must be remembered that this Church was erected for the Latin service; that when it was finished a convent of Augustinian Canons was placed in possession of the whole; and that after the Latins were driven out by Saladin, the Greeks obtained this choir, and have retained it ever since. Accordingly it is now fitted in their manner with a huge *Iconostasis*, or screen with three doors, cutting off the apse and half the remainder of the presbytery where the high altar is placed, and having its side tables against the piers from whence the apse springs. But, apart from these characteristics, the Altar (38) stands evidently on its Latin site upon the diametral line of the apse; and the Greek choral stalls under the lantern cupola are in the very position that the Latins would have placed them, and probably did so[3].

[3] The length of the choir and presbytery together, from the screen to the apse wall, is ninety-eight feet, and the breadth is forty feet, more or less.

The western screen is fixed under the western arch (4) of the lantern, and divides the choir from the Rotunda, communicating on the same level with the platform which leads to the Holy Sepulchre.

In the middle of the choir, the writer in Beugnot places a lectern of marble, called *le Compas*, where the Epistle was read. But Sæwulf tells us that the place called *Compas* was at the *Caput*, or extremity of the Round Church of the Sepulchre, and was held to be the centre of the world: an absurdity which is retained to the present day[1]. The extremity of the Rotunda, as it stood in Sæwulf's time, exactly coincides with the middle of the Crusaders' choir. This supposed centre is first mentioned by Bernardus (A.D. 870)[1].

The western arch (4) which connects the Rotunda with the choir, is described by Quaresmius as having been decorated with mosaic work, of which sufficient remained to shew that above it, to the west, was a representation of the Annunciation, apparently in the spandrils of the arch, one containing the figure of the Angel, and the other that of the Virgin. The soffit itself had a mosaic of the Ascension, with inscriptions in Greek and Latin. The eastern apse and the vault of the choir were also decorated with mosaics of figures on gilt grounds.

The apse had four double pillars sustaining pointed

---

[1] This tradition appears to originate from a strange interpretation of the following passage of the Psalms, which is quoted by the various authors on this subject. Psal. lxxiii. 12: "Deus autem Rex noster ante sæcula, operatus est salutem in medio terræ;" or, in our version, Ps. lxxiv. 12: "For God is my King of old, working salvation in the midst of the earth." Fabri tells an amusing story of one of his companions who paid a large sum for permission to ascend to the top of the cupola, in order to satisfy himself if he were really over the centre of the earth, by observing whether or no the sun gave him a shadow at noon.

arches and resting upon seven marble gradations, which occupied the whole semicircle like a theatre; and on their summit, at the eastern extremity, and under the eastern central arch, was placed the marble chair of the Patriarch. The pavement was of the best and most ornate workmanship, and had an altar in the midst, of elaborate construction, decorated with precious marbles and small columns, but these had been so battered by the infidels, that Quaresmius relates there were scarcely left fragments enough to shew what it had once been. A smaller Altar, after the Greek fashion (namely the Altar of Prothesis), was placed on the north side (39), near the pier in advance of the High Altar, and dedicated to the three Kings.

On each side, and against the eastern piers of the tower, were two platforms (40, 41), each ascended by four steps, and each originally intended to receive two (or, as some say, one) marble Patriarchal chair. These four chairs, according to the Greeks, were provided for the four Patriarchs of Constantinople, Alexandria, Antioch, and Jerusalem.

An aisle surrounds the presbytery and apse, communicating on each side with the transepts, and forming the usual procession-path of the Romanesque Churches. Three apsidal Chapels radiate from the aisle, and alternating with them are four doors, as shewn in the Plan[2]. Of the Chapels, the north-eastern (25) is dedicated to St Longinus; and here was formerly preserved a relic which was believed to be the actual title which Pilate affixed to the Cross[3]. The eastern Chapel (27) is called

[2] The chapels are marked, 25, 27, 34, and the doors 24, 26, 28, 35.

[3] This relic however was removed to Rome, where it may be seen in the

the Chapel of the Division of the Vestments; and the south-eastern (34), the Chapel of the Mocking; in the latter of which is preserved under the Altar a column reported to have been brought from the house of Pilate, and upon which the soldiers seated the Saviour when they crowned him with thorns and derided him[1]. Of the four doors above-mentioned, the first on the north (24) was formerly the passage from the Church to the Dormitory and Convent of the Canons in the time of the Crusaders. The second (26), in its original state, was probably a window. The third (28) leads by a descending stair to the Chapel of St Helena. And the fourth, the last (35) on the south, to an ascending stair which conducts to the apartments occupied by the Greeks.

But to return to the third door. This conducts by a long descending stair of thirty steps in a narrow passage partly formed in the rock, to the large Chapel dedicated to St Helena, the floor of which is fifteen feet nine inches below that of the Rotunda[2]. It is nearly square, being forty-three feet in width, and fifty-one in length from the foot of the stairs to the spring of the apse, which apse is six feet deep. The Chapel is divided into three aisles by two columns on each

church called "S. Croce in Gierusalemme." Quaresmius, T. II. p. 397. Longinus is the name given in the spurious Gospel of Nicodemus to the soldier who pierced the side of our Saviour, and is accepted by the Romish Church.

[1] Sæwulf, in 1102, enumerates the *locus* where the Cross was found, the marble column of Flagellation, the *locus* where the Lord was stripped of his garments, the *locus* where the purple robe and crown of thorns were put on, and where the soldiers cast lots for the vestments. As this passage was written before the Crusaders' Church was commenced, it appears that these *loci* are local, probably Syrian, traditions, and were accommodated by the Crusaders in the Plan of their apse, as explained above. They are not mentioned, however, by any other writers until the sixteenth century, as far as I have examined them.

[2] On the authority of Mr Scoles.

side. These carry pointed arches and a stone vault, but the central compartment rises into a cupola, having a low tambour and four windows, which are the only sources of light to the Chapel. There is an admirable view of the interior in Roberts' Palestine, which may be compared with one engraved in the "Univers." From these it seems that the architecture of this Chapel is massive, rude, and crypt-like, the columns of a dwarfish proportion, with capitals apparently of early Byzantine character, having the peculiar hemispherical form and reticulated ornament, surmounted by leaves, that often appears in that style. It was not affected by the fire of 1808.

This Chapel, in every respect in its plan, resembles a small Greek Church, having a narthex or vestibule at the west end separated from the rest of the Church by square cruciform piers, a cupola in the middle resting on four round pillars, and eastern apses (29, 30), which are in this case confined to two in number, on account of the steps (32) which descend to the Chapel of the Invention occupying the place usually assigned to the southern apse. Amongst Greek Churches many of a similar plan may be seen, as for example, La Martorana in Palermo, the Church of Kapnicarea at Athens, (Couchaud. Pl. 15), the Church of the Theotocos at Constantinople, and many others. The vaulting is, however, differently managed, and may have been reconstructed by the Crusaders. But I am of opinion that they found this Church in existence, and merely repaired and adapted it to their new building.

The want of symmetrical position with respect to the Crusaders' apse, and the intrusion of the stairs into the narthex[1], also shew that this Chapel was in existence before the apse of the great Church was planned.

The central altar is dedicated to St Helena, and the northern altar to the Good Thief, or to his cross[2]. On the North (31) side is a patriarchal chair of marble, usually said to be that in which Helena sat while they were digging in search of the Cross.

The southern aisle of the Chapel, in lieu of an apse, has a descending stair (32) of twelve steps, and a doorway which leads to an irregularly-shaped apartment (33), about twenty feet across, excavated in the rock[3], the floor of which is eleven feet below that of the Chapel of St Helena. The sides are disposed in the form of an irregular pentagon, and the low roof is partly artificial and partly formed by the overhanging rock. Quaresmius describes it as appearing to have been a reservoir of water. This is the place where the three Crosses, the crown of thorns and the nails, the title, &c. are supposed to have been found when the rubbish which had

---

[1] According to the minute Fabri, the sides of the passage, in which the descending staircase is placed, are cut in the rock, the surface of which still forms the walls thereof. But the steps themselves are of stone; also the walls of the chapel itself are rock. "Hæc capella est satis magna, alias parietes non habens nisi petras, in quibus est incisa; sicut et ipsi gradus de superiori ecclesia *inter parietes petrarum* descendunt," (p. 293.) He had just stated that this descent was by "*gradus lapideos.*" Quaresmius (p. 408) makes them 29 steps, "ex dolata marmore elaborati." In fact, the site of the chapel is a rectangular, dry cistern, as it were, sunk in the rock, and the passage formed in an artificial cleft, cut into the western side of this cistern. In the original construction, I imagine the stairs were set farther west in this cleft, so as to leave the narthex free. Now, the steps are driven so far east by the Crusaders' apse, that they occupy the whole of the center of the narthex.

[2] Quaresmius, p. 423.

[3] Richardson describes it as a low rocky vault and a murky den, large enough to contain thirty or forty persons wedged in close array. Vol. II. p. 325.

accumulated in this cavern was cleared out under the superintendence of St Helena A.D. 326 or 327. The apartment is accordingly named the *Chapel of the Invention of the Cross;* and in the North-eastern corner an altar is placed in a rude apse upon the spot where the supposed Cross lay hid for three centuries.

On the North side of the descent is a fissure of the rock, which is quoted by some as one of the rents that accompanied the Crucifixion, but which Quaresmius declares to be manifestly an artificial opening, and no other than the proper canal or conduit which belonged to the original employment of this cavern as a cistern. As another instance of the tendency to explain every appearance about this spot in miraculous connexion with the events commemorated there, the dew-drops that naturally hang on the surface of the damp walls and columns, were believed by the pilgrims to be tears shed by the very stones in sympathy with the events that took place on this spot.

The above description of the East end of the Church, with its chapels and appendages, may be compared with that given in Beugnot[4], which explains admirably the arrangement of the Convent of the Canons.

"At the *chevet* or apse of the choir there was a door on the right hand, by which the Canons entered to

[4] Assises de Jerusalem, Tome II. p. 531. Schultz's Jerusalem, p. 109. "Au cheves dou cuer avoit une porte, par là où li chanoine entroient en leur offecines, à mein destre. Entre cele porte et mont de Calvaire avoit I. mout parfont fossé, où en avaloit à degres. Là avoit une place que en apeloit *Sainte Helaine*. Là trouva Sainte Helainne la crois et les clous et le martel et la courone....Tout ainsi que li chanoine issoient dou sepulcre, à mein senestre estoit leur dortoirs, et à mein destre li refrotois et tenoit au mont de Calvarie. Entre ces II. offices estoit leur clistres et leur preaus. En un lieu du peel avoit une grant ouverture, dont on veoit en la chambre Elaine qui dessous estoit, car autrement n'i veoit on goute."

their apartments. Between this door and Mount Calvary was a door or passage, excavated downwards to some depth, where there were steps, and at the bottom a place called of *Sainte Helaine,* and there S. Helaine found the cross, and the nails, and the hammer, and the crown. ....And when the Canons issued from the Sepulchre, on the left was their dortoir, and on the right their refectory, against the Mount of Calvary. Between these two offices was their cloister, with the *preau* or court in the midst. In one place of this building was a great opening, through which could be seen the chamber of Helaine below, and this was all that could be seen of it."

At present the space at the East end of the Church is occupied by a Coptic Convent, and, according to the description given me by Mr Williams of their buildings, I conjecture that they must contain the remains of the very dormitory and cloister above described; for to this day their court is formed upon the roof of the chapel of St Helena, the cupola of which rises in the middle, and through its windows a view may be had of the chapel below, as Beugnot describes. On the South side a wall with pointed arches must clearly be the ruins of the refectory; and on the North of that is a flourishing olive-tree, which is believed to be the very tree in which Abraham found a ram caught by the horns.

But, to return to the interior of the Church. It will be remembered that the choir is placed under a central lantern cupola, and has a transept to the North and South. The North transept of the Church presents nothing remarkable, and I will therefore proceed to describe the parts that lie to the South of the choir. The South transept has several irregularities in its arrangement, which arise from the earlier buildings which already existed when it was erected, and to which its plan was made subservient. The Chapels of Mount Calvary, which lie on its eastern side, are those which have principally affected it.

The central portions of the Church are constructed in the usual manner in three stories, namely, pier-arch, triforium, and clerestory. The floor of the triforium is about thirty-three feet above the pavement of the Church. The triforium-gallery runs not only along the east and west walls of the South transept, but also across its southern wall. This south wall of the transept contains a double-arched doorway (55, 56), and is indeed now the only entrance-front of the Church. On the inside, opposite to the middle pier of the door, is placed a double column, which supports the arches and vault that carry the triforium-gallery across the South end of this transept[1].

The eastern wall of the transept has three arches between the lantern-pier and the south wall. The most northerly of these arches (46) is as high as the other pier-arches of the Church, and opens to the side-aisle or procession-path of the presbytery. But the other two arches are much lower, for behind them an intermediate vault is introduced, carrying a floor only fifteen feet above the pavement of the Church.

This intermediate or mezzanine floor extends considerably to the East; and by comparing the plan of it (Fig. 5) with the ground-plan of that part of the Church which lies below it, this somewhat complex arrangement will be evident[2].

---

[1] In the north transept the triforium gallery runs over the ancient cloister (21).

[2] The section in Fig. 10, Plate 3, will explain the manner in which the surface of the Rock forms part of the floor of the upper chapels, and how this floor is carried on westward by means of the vaults.

The mezzanine floor comprises two principal chapels, called the *Chapel of the Exaltation of the Cross* (72, 73), and the *Chapel of the Crucifixion* (71), respectively; also a small lateral building (70) or porch, by which a flight of steps (54) descends to the court, so as to give independent access to the chapels from without. On the East side are some buildings occupied by the Greeks, and two small chapels (74), called the *Chapels of Abraham and Melchisedech*. The whole of this eastern appendage, and part of the Chapel of the Exaltation, rests upon the surface of the rock, which rises so high above the rest of the Church, as to form a pavement on the level of the mezzanine floor. But the remainder of the Chapel of the Exaltation and the entire Chapel of the Crucifixion, together with the porch, have their pavements (the mezzanine floor) supported by the intermediate vault, and beneath them the space is occupied by a Chapel (47) which has received different names, out of which we may select that of the *Chapel of Adam;* and also by two other apartments (51, 52), and a small chapel (53) under the porch. We may now examine these chapels in detail, and begin with the North chapel of the mezzanine floor.

About nine feet of the eastern end of the floor of this chapel is rock, which rises slightly above the general level, and has its upper surface covered with white marble slabs, which raise it altogether two feet above the pavement. Three feet from the front of this raised part and in the centre, is situated the hole, which is said to be the very hole in which the foot of the Cross was planted. The cavity is about two feet deep and six inches in diameter, but was lined and garnished with silver plates[1].

[1] Quaresmius gives an engraving and various particulars of this decoration: the plates bore date 1560. The chapel is fifteen feet seven inches wide

An altar is placed above it, and the chapel is in the custody of the Greeks.

Two other holes are situated, the one to the right and the other to the left of the central one, and six feet nine inches distant from it, measured from centre to centre. They are set in a line about eighteen inches farther eastward than the middle one.

Notwithstanding their proximity, they are believed to have been made to receive the crosses of the thieves: the good thief to the north, the bad thief to the south[2].

This chapel (72, 73) is termed by the Latins the *Chapel of the Exaltation of the Cross*, to distinguish it from the neighbouring chapel (71) on its south side, which they call the *Chapel of the Crucifixion*, asserting that the Body was nailed to the Cross in the south

---

between the piers, and thirty-six feet long. On the north side of the chapel a staircase (45) led down to the side-aisle of the choir, and was the only access to this floor after the original external porch and stairs were blocked up by the Mohammedans. But since the fire of 1808 the space of these chapels has been enlarged by the addition of a gallery in front of the western wall, projecting nine feet into the south transept. This gallery contains two staircases, apparently for the convenience of conducting the crowd of pilgrims up one, and down the other, in order. Also the intermediate floor of Calvary has been extended into the south aisle of the choir, which is now completely covered by it, from its opening in the south transept to the chapel of the Mocking, thus forming a convenient access from the chapel of the Exaltation of the Cross, which belongs to the Greeks, to their kitchen behind, and to their other dwelling apartments, which are above the kitchen, and also, by means of stairs, to their choir. A small gangway appears always to have existed between the small door near the foot-hole of the Cross and the Greek kitchen. This is seen in the section, Plate 3. The fire broke out in the Armenian Church, which is in the western triforium of the south transept (over 68), opposite to the Chapels of Calvary; and consequently so damaged those Chapels and the whole transept as to necessitate much rebuilding, restoration, and change, by which their venerable and ancient character has been wholly destroyed.

[2] In all probability, the three holes were originally made to receive a *representation* of the Crucifixion. The south chapel is narrower than the other, (thirteen feet three inches wide,) but about the same length.

chapel, and the Cross afterwards raised up and fixed in the hole of the northern chapel.

The south chapel (71) is, nevertheless, an upper floor, raised upon a vault, and the apartment below it is used for a vestry, and appears to be held in no veneration whatever. This anomaly is alluded to by Quaresmius[1], and he suggests that the earth beneath the pavement has been removed for the convenience of the structure, or because St Helena conveyed it to Rome, so that the spot above, upon which he would have us believe the crucifixion to have taken place, is yet in the true position in space, although the ground has been taken from under it. But, in fact, this especial tradition is not mentioned by any of the pilgrim-writers, until long after the expulsion of the Crusaders; and the probable explanation of its history is, that when the Latins, upon their return to the Church in 1257, found the Greeks in possession of the hole in the rock and its chapel, they set up a claim in the side-chapel to a spot of similar sanctity in connexion with the events that took place on this locality. And the same may be said of the absurd tradition mentioned below, that places the witnesses of the Crucifixion upon the upper landing of the porch which was built by the Crusaders.

The two chapels, as well as the porch, were elaborately decorated with mosaic-work and pavements of marble. These chapels, especially the northern one, suffered exceeding damage from the fire of 1808; for immediately to the East, on the spot marked (75) as

[1] Notandum, locum istum subtus excavatum esse, et non ob id negandum, verè locum esse crucifixionis; nam id ita accidit, tum quia terra sacri montis ab Helena Romam asportata fuit, tum quia alia adhibita pro templi structura. (Quar. 444.)

the Greek kitchen, there stood a wooden building in the form of a tower, in six or seven stories, which served as a dwelling for the Greeks in charge of the Church, and of course fell an immediate prey to the flames[2]. The porch (70) on the right hand of the entrance-doors in the court, is in the form of an elegant turret, in two stories, surmounted by a cupola. It is in the same style as the front of the Church, and evidently the work of the Crusaders. The upper story has rich pointed arches, which were apparently open in the original design. This story, the floor of which is on a level with that of the chapels of the Exaltation of the Cross and of the Crucifixion, was intended for a vestibule to them, and the external staircase (54) still remains which led to this upper floor. The vestibule itself, not ten feet square, has had an altar placed in it at some modern period, and is dignified as the place or station where the Virgin and St John stood during the Crucifixion; and hence is called the Chapel of the Virgin and St John the Evangelist. The first mention, however, of such a station, is by Sæwulf and the anonymous chronicler of the Crusaders[3]. They fix its position at the altar of Sta Maria Latina—a Church known to have stood on the south side of the street that bounds the front court of the Church of the Sepulchre. The location of this *station* in the porch at the stair-head, occurs in the later pilgrim-writers only; and it may be supposed, that when the Christians lost Jerusalem, and the Church of Sta Maria Latina was ruined and abandoned, the *station* was removed to the porch. It is mentioned very doubtfully by most of these writers, and there

[2] Account of the fire by the Latin monks in Turner's Levant.

[3] Recueil de Voyages. Tom. IV. p. 842. Gesta Dei per Francos, p. 573.

seems to be some confusion between this chapel and the neighbouring Chapel of Adam, to which the same dedication is assigned[1]. The lower story (53) of the porch is converted into a chapel of the fourth-century saint called Maria Egyptiaca.

Having now described the chapels of the mezzanine floor, it remains to examine the vaults below them. Of these, the southern vaults (51, 52) were apparently never used as chapels; but the northern vault (47) has been already mentioned as the Chapel of Adam. A little consideration will shew that this chapel is placed immediately beneath the western brow of the rock, near the margin of which above, is the so-called foot-hole of the Cross. This is best seen in the section, Fig. 10; and in the general plan of the Church, Plate 2, the position of this hole is marked with a circle. The chapel has an apse at its eastern extremity, and the apse is described by all travellers, ancient and modern, as being hewn out of a rock and not constructed of masonry. Moreover, there is a fissure in the face of it, which also appears in the rocky surface above, close to the south side of the foot-hole[2]. This fissure is of course appealed to as having been formed when "the rocks were rent" at the Crucifixion. It is easy to see that this projecting rock must have been artificially squared on its western face, which contains the apse, and also on its northern and southern faces; so that if the buildings were

[1] To a much later period belong two similar stations, which are, or were, marked in the pavement by circular stones, the one in the south apsidal chapel (5) of the Rotunda, said to be the spot where Mary Magdalene and others "beheld where He was laid," the other in the aisle of the Rotunda (68), opposite the Stone of Unction, where the "acquaintance and the women stood afar off beholding." (Quaresmius, T. I. p. 496.) They are not mentioned by any early writer.

[2] This is exhibited by means of a hole left for the purpose in the pavement.

removed, it would now appear like a wedge, rising gradually from the east; and bounded by these artificial vertical surfaces on the three sides of its western extremity. This shall be examined presently, when the description of the buildings has been concluded. In the middle ages, the term Calvary was applied to the entire surface of this hill, extending from the place of Crucifixion to the Chapel of St Helena and of the Invention; but the term Golgotha was limited to the spot immediately below the western brow of Calvary, which we are now considering, or at least only included in addition the upper edge of this brow, where the Cross was planted. The chapel is said by Quaresmius to have its vault decorated with mosaic work, and its pavement with marble slabs and tesselation. There is a small altar in the apse. Bernardino denominates it the Chapel of Godfrey, from one of its most remarkable characteristics, namely, that it was chosen as a sepulchral chapel by the first Crusading kings of Jerusalem[3], who thus chose their resting-place at the foot of their Saviour's Cross. The tomb of Godfrey de Bouillon, the first king, stood at the entrance of the chapel (48) against the north pier, and

---

[3] The expressions made use of by Will. of Tyre shew that, in his time, the term *Golgotha* was restricted to the lower ground immediately in front of the Rock upon which the Cross was fixed, to which the term *Calvary* was appropriated. King Baldwin..."sepultus est inter prædecessores suos piæ recordationis Reges sub Monte Calvariæ ante locum qui dicitur Golgotha." W. Tyr. Lib. XIII. p. 851; also Lib. II. p. 816. Sæwulf also mentions "Mons Calvariæ ... subtus est locus qui Golgotha dicitur." The dedication or title of this chapel is somewhat uncertain. Arculfus alludes to it, but gives it no name; but Epiphanius tells us that "Beneath Calvary is the church and tomb of Adam," and Quaresmius calls it the Chapel of Adam. The name has reference to a strange, but early, tradition that Adam was buried under Mount Calvary. This tradition is mentioned and condemned by Jerome, (Comm. in Matth. Lib. IV. c. 27,) and other early ecclesiastical writers. But the pilgrims Breydenbach, Zuallardo, and Cotovicus, not

the tomb of Baldwin I. (49), his brother and successor, exactly similar to it, against the south pier. Other kings were entombed against the south wall of enclosure of the choir. But these sepulchral monuments were subsequently defaced and injured by the Charizmians in 1244, as already described; and by the Greeks[1] because they commemorated Latin sovereigns; and it seems that, in the late restoration, they have been wholly destroyed or obliterated, from a similar motive[2].

In the pavement of the South transept there is a remarkable stone (50) fixed, not in the middle of the transept, but rather opposite to the middle of the present entrance-door. This, which appears simply to have been an ordinary marble slab, probably the

only say that the head of Adam was found here, but some (as Bernardino) would have us believe that it is still to be seen in the fissure of the apse. In the Greek Pilgrim's Guide it is termed the Chapel of St John *Baptist*, and of Adam. Breydenbach, the Count of Solms, (1483,) and others, denominate this the Chapel of the Virgin Mary and St John. Zuallardo, the Chapel of St John the Evangelist and of the Unction; and Cotovicus, the Chapel of St John the Evangelist. Remembering the prominent position which the Virgin and St John occupy in all mediæval representations of the Crucifixion, in which they are always placed one on each side of the Cross, we need not be surprised to find a chapel dedicated to them immediately at the foot of the Cross.

[1] Quaresmius, 483.

[2] See De Géramb's Pilgrimage, which contains a good account of the fire and its consequences. The best representation of the two monuments of Godfrey and Baldwin is given by Zuallardo. They were alike, with the exception that the first had twisted columns, and the second plain, and the design consisted simply of a roof-shaped stone of fine porphyry, with vertical gable ends, and ornamented on its edge with carving and moldings. The inscription was placed on the sloping surface. The stone is supported upon four dwarf columns, two feet six inches in height, which rest on a base or plinth of marble, about a foot high, of the same horizontal dimensions as the upper stone, that is to say, eight feet by four. Within the chapel, on the right hand of the entrance, is a sarcophagus of white marble, which the Greeks say is the tomb of Melchisedech. The screen-wall, which contained the door of this chapel, projected into the south transept, so as to enclose the tombs of the kings, as shewn by the dotted lines in Plate 2.

covering of a grave, from its dimensions (about six feet by three[3]), has been raised to the dignity of the *Stone of Unction*, upon which they say the Lord's Body was laid when it was taken from the Cross and anointed. It is said to be a green-coloured stone, but a slab of white marble has been cemented upon it, to protect it from the depredations of the pilgrims, and borders of mosaic work set round it, with an iron railing and candlesticks. It is the first object that meets the eye upon entering the church.

The earliest mention of the place of Unction is by Sæwulf, who says that "close to the place of Calvary is the church of Sancta Maria in the place where the Lord's Body, when taken down from the Cross, was wrapped up in a linen cloth with spices." He fixes this church or chapel in the atrium of the Rotunda on the East side, to distinguish it from those on the West side.

This church of St Mary therefore must be the small oratory over the place of Unction which is mentioned by William of Tyre, and also the quadrangular church of St Mary which Arculfus places in contact with the right (South) side of the Rotunda. As the Crusaders found this station established as one of the Holy Places, they probably did not essentially alter its position, and we may infer that the Church of St Mary stood on the site of the present South transept. The place is first mentioned as a *stone* (a black stone) by Rudolph von Suchem in 1336[4]. But it seems that a purplish stone, said to have been employed for the same purpose, had been long preserved at Ephesus, from whence it was conveyed to Constantinople by the Emperor Manuel

[3] Palmi otto lungo e quattro largo. (Bernardino, p. 32.)

[4] Reyssbuch der Heil. L. p. 844.

(c. 1150)[1]. The present stone is probably a paving-stone originally laid over some spot of the rock that became reputed as the "*locus Unctionis,*" and subsequently the stone itself became covered up with another stone to preserve it[2].

The South or principal entrance-front of the Church, which is, as we have seen, the wall of the South transept, has been so repeatedly drawn and engraved of late years by competent artists, that its appearance has become familiarised to us all. It is a pointed Romanesque composition, which derives a peculiar character from its being attached to a flat-roofed building. The lower story is occupied by a wide double doorway with detached shafts supporting carved and molded arches, with a sculptured hoodmold. The outer order of voussoirs has a radiating ornament, which occurs, amongst other examples, in the Church of the Martorana in Sicily. The second order of voussoirs is richly molded, and the inner shafts carry a transom ornamented with sculpture. The western door (56) is the only one that remains open at present, the eastern (55) has been walled up, apparently ever since the Mohammedans expelled the Crusaders.

In the upper story are two rich windows, of similar decorations to the doorways below. But their arches

---

[1] Nicetas, Lib. VII.; Quaresm. p. 493; Du Cange Constantinopolis Christiana, p. 81, Lib. IV. He placed it in the church of the Pantocrator at Constantinople, and near his own sepulchre.

[2] The place, according to Quaresmius, was in the sixteenth century still ornamented with a rich mosaic work, and the stone itself was of a greenish colour. Breydenbach does not allude to the Unction, but in stead mentions a place, marked with a white stone, where the Mater Dolorosa sat, with the dead Body of her Son in her bosom taken from the Cross. But his cotemporary, Fabri, describes, in his peculiar way, his horror and remorse at discovering, upon his first entry into this Church, that he had inadvertently trampled upon the stone of Unction.

are so slightly pointed, that the hoodmolds are very nearly semicircular. The string-courses of this front are richly sculptured.

The western side of this court is formed by the campanile and the range of chapels with polygonal apses already described, and the southern side retains the bases of a row of columns that once belonged to a cloister or portico. They stand on the top of a flight of steps that rise from, and extend entirely across, the court. On this South side of the court originally stood the buildings of the Knights Hospitallers, and the monasteries, male and female, of Sancta Maria Latina, the history of which will be found in another part of this volume.

The western side of the court is occupied by a range of buildings, probably of no great antiquity, and in this side are three doors, of which the most northerly (57), close to the chapel of the porch, opens to a chapel dedicated to St Michael and All Saints, in possession of the Copts, and through which is the passage to their convent, which, as already described, occupies part of the site of the Crusaders' convent of Canons. The middle door (58) opens to an Armenian Church of St John[3], and the southern door (59) to the Greek monastery of Abraham, which derives its name from the Chapel of Abraham's Sacrifice, attached to these buildings.

One of the ancient traditions of this spot is that this sacrifice took place upon the mount of Calvary, and Antoninus Placentinus enumerates the place where

[3] Of S. John the Baptist, according to W. Wey, Saligniaco, Breydenbach, and Quaresmius; but the Pilgrim's Guide of Chrysanthus makes it of S. John the Evangelist.

Abraham sacrificed, and that where he was met by Melchisedech, amongst those which were visited by the Pilgrims by the side of the place of Crucifixion. Arculfus and Sæwulf only mention the first. However, these two localities are still indicated by two Altars in a small Chapel (74) constructed behind the Chapels of Calvary[1]. They are reached by means of a narrow passage and staircase leading through the Greek convent of Abraham; and, to complete the list, the pilgrim is shewn the ancient olive at the back of the buildings, which he is told is the tree in which Abraham's ram was caught by the horns[2].

IX.

THE ORIGINAL FORM OF THE GROUND.

I HAVE now conducted my reader through the buildings that surround the Holy Sepulchre, and must endeavour, in the next place, to investigate the probable form of the rocky surface, as it existed before the buildings of Constantine and those that followed them were undertaken.

For it is evidently shewn by the traces of hewn rock that we have encountered in various parts of our survey, as, for example, in the tomb called of Joseph of Arimathæa, in the Prison, in the Chapel of St Helena and the stairs that lead to it, in the Chapel of the Invention, on Calvary, and in the Chapel of Adam, not to mention the Holy Sepulchre itself[3]; by all these examples, I say, it

[1] These are not exactly laid down upon any of the plans, but by description must be located in the space indicated in my plan at (74).

[2] Quaresmius, T. I. p. 281; Zuallardo, &c.

[3] Vide Plate 2, Nos. 1, 6, 23, 28, 30, 33, 72, 47.

is shewn that the site, originally rough and rocky, must have been levelled into platforms for the reception of the first buildings that were erected here; and it is necessary that we should endeavour to discover what the natural form of the ground was. Plate I. Fig. 1, is intended to illustrate this point, and I shall refer to it throughout this Section; I have traced upon it the outlines of the principal buildings, namely, the Chapel of Helena at the east end, and the aisle-wall of the Rotunda at the west with its three apses; also the Prison on the north; and the apse of the Chapel of Adam with the outline of the three vertical faces which at present bound the rock of Calvary on the south. I have also added the four streets which in the present town enclose the site. Upon these I have endeavoured to represent the original undulating surface.

The area is bounded by four streets, namely, Sepulchre Street on the north, Palmer Street on the south, Patriarch Street on the west, and St Stephen Street on the east. Sepulchre Street had at its eastern extremity (I) the Porta Judiciaria, of which a column still remains to shew the position, and this street is described as a steep regular ascent from I to K; which, considering the length of the street, would place K about thirty feet higher than I[4].

Patriarch Street is described as descending very gently and imperceptibly from north to south (from K to L). But at the point L, those who wish to reach the Church of the Sepulchre turn off from Patriarch Street, and after passing through a narrow lane (L M) with

---

[4] For Sepulchre Street is 360 feet in length, from I to K, which, if the mean inclination be one in twelve, would give thirty feet for the elevation of K above I. One in twelve is by no means a very steep ascent.

several crooked turnings and a steep descent with steps, find themselves at the South end of the court of the Church, where, as we have already seen, was once a cloister. From this point three steps more lead down to the court and into the Church. Thus it is evident that the gradual slope of the Northern street is compensated for in the Southern street by a rapid descent with many steps, which shews that something like the brow of a cliff is situated between Patriarch Street and the court of the Church, for Palmer Street (M G) from this court to St Stephen Street appears to be tolerably level, and so also is St Stephen Street from G to I, or at least their slope is a mere gentle inclination downwards towards the south-east. It follows from this, that the pavement of the Rotunda lies at about the same level as the Street of St Stephen, and that the point of Patriarch Street, which lies in contact with the Rotunda, cannot be less than from twenty to twenty-five feet above that pavement. I have already shewn that the western door of the Rotunda gave admission to the triforium of the Church; and it seems that in the original state of the ground this abrupt slope at L must have extended northwards, forming the rugged brow of a cliff, in which the cave of the Holy Sepulchre C and the catacomb D (of which the so-called tomb of Joseph and Nicodemus was a part) were excavated. The architects of Constantine must have cut away the rock on the south, west, and north sides of the Sepulchral cavern, leaving it standing in a manner analogous to that in which the tombs of Absalom and Zachariah were detached from the rock that lies behind them[1].

[1] Mr Fergusson, in a passage distinguished by his usual felicity of expression and good taste, informs us that "the out-and-out advocates for the

So far therefore from the cave having been originally formed in an isolated rock that stood up from the level land, as it is usually represented[2], the present state of the ground shews that this Sepulchre was excavated out of the face of the cliff like the common tombs of Jerusalem and elsewhere, described in the second section above; and that its conversion into an isolated monolith was the work of Constantine. And this explains very readily the concealment and preservation

---

identity of the present Sepulchre insist that it is a cave in a rock, but that the rock has been cased with stone, inside and out; as however, according to all the plans I have had access to, Mr Williams' among others, the rock, with its casing, is in some places only two feet thick, and nowhere more than five, and the casing cannot be less than nine inches to a foot on each side, it would have been easier for the impious men to have removed it *in toto*, than to have covered it up: half-a-dozen men would have accomplished the job in a week," p. 88. The text, to which this passage is appended as a note, shews that by the "impious men" he means those mentioned by Eusebius, as having covered up the Cave to conceal it, and to afford a foundation for the Temple of Venus. Mr Fergusson can scarcely require to be informed that the advocates for the identity of the present Sepulchre necessarily suppose it to have been wrought, by Constantine's orders, into such a form externally as would enable it to receive the ornamental casing; as indeed S. Cyril implies in the passage quoted, amongst others, by Mr Williams, in the first edition of the Holy City, p. 295; and although it is quite true that by *this process* the thickness of rock and casing has been in some places brought down to less than three feet at the western corners of the chamber, it is equally clear that the state of it must have been very different when "the impious men" operated upon it two centuries before, in the time of Hadrian. Indeed, I have endeavoured to shew that it was only brought to its present form by a very laborious excavation. Mr. Fergusson's supposition of from nine inches to a foot for the thickness of the casing, would be true if it were an ashlaring of stone, but it is a lastrication of marble slabs, for which three or four inches is an ample allowance.

[2] Eusebius, in the Theophania, evidently describes the Cave as he saw it, after the operations of Constantine had taken place. "It is astonishing to see even this rock standing out erect and alone, in a level land, and having only one cavern within it." Book III. p. 199, of Lee's translation. If the above supposition be rejected, we must conclude that the Sepulchre of the Gospels was originally detached from the Rock, like those of Absalom and Zachariah; but the latter are evidently Pagan tombs, and not Jewish.

of it when the agents of Hadrian heaped earth upon it and erected a Temple of Venus thereon; an operation of no difficulty, since they had only to cover up an opening in front of the cliff[1].

But the rock of Calvary at E still stands up fifteen feet above the pavement, and it appears likely that in its original state this rock was part of a little swell of the ground that jutted out from the slope of Sepulchre Street, and probably always formed a somewhat abrupt brow on the West and South sides. This would afford a convenient spot for the place of public execution. For the south-western brow of the rock has just sufficient elevation to raise the wretched sufferers above the gazing crowd, that would naturally arrange itself below and upon the sloping ridge opposite (at M), which formed a kind of natural theatre with respect to the brow of Calvary.

The ground immediately to the West of St Stephen Street (G I) appears at present to have accumulated. In its original state I have supposed it to have sloped down gradually eastward from the brow of Calvary and the little isthmus, F E, which connected that hill with the main slope of Sepulchre Street. It must be remembered that the city wall, G I, formed the West boundary of St Stephen Street, according to the accounts of those who defend the authenticity of the present Holy Sepulchre, and with which I concur. The ground, however, between the Chapel of Helena (A) and this wall, is higher than St Stephen Street, and is bounded by an abrupt descent, described as a

[1] Fabri (p. 326) imagines that the opening of the outer cave of the Sepulchre looked to the south, which is not impossible, and not inconsistent with the view I have given above of the original state of the ground.

bank of earth (not of rock), which shews its South face behind a certain tannery in Palmer Street (at N), and its eastern face between the Chapel of Helena and the street, and upon this bank is erected the Coptic Convent, formerly the Convent of the Canons of the Sepulchre. The part of the street of St Stephen occupied by a deserted bazar, is arched over (from H to I), and the raised ground is so much higher than the street at this point, that the garden-surface is carried over these arches without interruption, so that this end of the street appears like a tunnel or excavation. But this accumulation is plainly the natural result of the form of the ground, which sloped downwards to the wall, and, occupied by buildings that have fallen into decay, would necessarily become heaped up in the corner, so as to admit of being levelled and formed into gardens[2].

X.

THE BASILICA OF CONSTANTINE.

Eusebius relates[3] that Constantine, being desirous to do honour to the place of our Lord's Resurrection, at Jerusalem, commanded an House of Prayer to be erected on that spot. For that certain impious persons

---

[2] That this ground is an accumulation, is evident from Schultz's description of the ruined portal, (which I shall presently shew was the great porch of Constantine's Basilica,) for he tells us that the pillars are half-buried in the ground, and that the bank of earth upon which the Abyssinian monastery stands rises behind them.

[3] The work of Eusebius is so well known, that it is unnecessary for me to do more in this place than give such a mere abridgment of his narrative, as may serve to introduce the description of the Basilica, which I shall translate at length.

(acting, as other authorities inform us, under the orders of the Emperor Hadrian[1],) had formerly resolved to consign to oblivion that Salutary Cave, and had therefore with much labour brought thither a vast quantity of earth, with which they filled up and levelled the whole place, and having paved it with stone, they thus concealed the Holy Cave beneath this heap of materials. They proceeded, moreover, to erect thereon a temple of Venus, and offered there their sacrifices. But the Emperor Constantine commanded that not only the buildings and the statues should be taken down, but that their materials, and even the earth which had been heaped up there, should all be carried away to a great distance, because they had been defiled with the blood of the profane sacrifices. When this was done, it was discovered, contrary to all expectation, that the Sepulchral Cavern existed unharmed beneath. Then the Emperor ordered a magnificent House of Prayer to be erected round about the Salutary Cave, and wrote letters to the governors of the Eastern provinces to forward the work, and amongst others, a letter (A. D. 326) to Macarius, the Bishop of Jerusalem, which is given at length by Eusebius, in which he expresses his joy and gratitude and admiration that the Token of our Saviour's most Holy Passion, for so many years hid under the earth, should now so gloriously appear; and confessing this to be miraculous, he declares his firm determination that that Holy Place which he had disburthened of the vile idol, should be ornamented with magnificent structures[2].

---

[1] Holy City, Vol. I. p. 240. Vol. II. p. 71.

[2] Writers who are interested in proving the authenticity of that wondrous relic which is known by the name of "the true Cross," endeavour to shew

He then exhorts the Bishop to provide all things necessary to enrich the beauty and excellence of this Basilica. He tells him that he has confided the substructures and decoration of the walls to Dracilianus, the deputy prefect, and to the president of the province, and has desired them to furnish workmen and artificers, and every thing that the Bishop may wish for, desiring moreover to be informed by him what columns and marbles may be requisite. And for the inner roof, which may be panelled, or otherwise ornamented, he suggests that if panelled, it should be gilt.

Eusebius in the next place presents us with a description of the buildings, which, like most written descriptions of architectural works, is exceedingly difficult to understand: for the writer was unacquainted with architecture, and hence great obscurity and want of precision prevails throughout. It can only be made tolerably intelligible, by a comparison with the site, and by considering the arrangement of other buildings of Constantine. I will first endeavour to translate the description, and then to explain it.

---

that Eusebius meant to allude to it in this letter, by the phrase "the token of the Passion," (*τὸ γνώρισμα τοῦ ἁγιωτάτου ἐκείνου πάθους.*) But when this solitary sentence is compared with the entire narrative before and after this place, it must be concluded that, however ill-chosen the expression may appear, no other is meant by it than the Cave. For it is clear, throughout the previous narrative, that when the first design of erecting a Martyrium upon this spot was conceived, it was not supposed that the Cave itself had remained uninjured, and that the discovery of it was so unexpected that its preservation was deemed miraculous. The Emperor's letter is written in accordance with these feelings, and with the previous history; and in the description of the buildings which follows, the whole arrangement is made subservient to the Cave, and there is not a word or allusion to the Cross, or even to Calvary. I believe therefore that the "token of the Passion" in this place is the Cave, which, as the scene of the crowning event of the Passion, may well have been termed one of the witnesses to it, by a florid writer like Eusebius.

Book III. Of the Life of Constantine.

Ch. 34. *Of the Holy Sepulchre.*

First, the Emperor's magnificence decorated the Sacred Cave itself, as the head of the whole work, with choice columns and great decoration, and ornamented it in every possible manner.

Ch. 35. *Of the Court and Cloisters.*

He then proceeded to *set in order* an extensive space open to the sky, which he paved with polished stones, and enclosed on three sides with long cloisters[1].

Ch. 36. *Of the Walls and Roof of the Basilica, and of the ornaments and gilding.*

On that side of the court which was situated opposite to the Cave, and towards the rising sun, was placed the Basilica[2]: an admirable work, raised to a mighty elevation, and extensive in length and breadth. Its interior was lined with many-coloured marbles, and the outer surface of its walls decorated with polished and closely-jointed masonry, as handsome as marble itself. The roof with its chambers was covered with lead, to protect it from the winter rains. The inner roof was decorated with sculptured panels, and extended like a vast sea over the whole Basilica; and being gilt with the purest gold, caused the entire building to shine as if with rays of light.

Ch. 37. *Of the Double Aisles on each side and of the three Eastern Doors.*

Moreover on either side, double piers of double porticoes[3], above and below ground, extended the full length of the temple, and their ceilings were gilt. Of these porticoes, those in front were sustained by enormous columns; those within, by square pilas-

---

[1] μακροῖς περιδρόμοις στοῶν: the Greek *stoa*, and the Latin *porticus*, appear to be best rendered in English by the word cloister. περίδρομος, a construction that admits of free passage round about a building, is introduced here to shew that the stoa or cloisters on the three sides were placed in continuous connexion with each other.

[2] ὁ βασίλειος νεώς.

[3] διττῶν στοῶν ἀναγείων τε καὶ καταγείων δίδυμοι παραστάδες.

ters or pedestals richly ornamented[4]. Three doors turned towards the rising sun admitted the entering crowd.

Ch. 38. *Of the Apse, and the twelve columns with capitals.*

Opposite to these doors was the apse[5], the head of the whole work, raised to the very roof of the Basilica. It was surrounded by twelve columns, the number of the Apostles; and they were ornamented with large silver capitals, which the Emperor dedicated to God as a beautiful gift.

Ch. 39. *Of the Atrium, the Exedræ, and the Portals.*

Hence, going forward to the entrances which were before the temple, he interposed an open space, *namely, between the Basilica and the portals:* there were also recessed chambers (exedræ) on each side, the first or entrance-court, which had cloisters attached to it, and lastly the gates of the court[6]. Beyond them, in the

---

[4] *ὧν αἱ μὲν ἐπὶ προσώπου τοῦ οἴκου, κίοσι παμμεγέθεσιν ἐπηρείδοντο· αἱ δ' εἴσω τῶν ἔμπροσθεν ὑπὸ πεσσοῖς ἀνηγείροντο, πολὺν τὸν ἔξωθεν περιβεβλημένοις κόσμον.*

[5] *ἡμισφαίριον.*

[6] Ἔκφρασις *μεσαυλείου καὶ ἐξεδρῶν καὶ προπύλων.* Ἔνθεν *δὲ προϊόντων ἐπὶ τὰς πρὸ τοῦ νεὼ κειμένας εἰσόδους, αἴθριον διελάμβανεν. ἦσαν δ' ἐνταυθοῖ παρ' ἑκάτερα, καὶ αὐλὴ πρώτη, στοαί τ' ἐπὶ ταύτῃ, καὶ ἐπὶ πᾶσιν αἱ αὔλειοι πύλαι.* This Chapter is the most obscure of the whole. Taken literally, as it stands in the Greek, it would place on each side of the Basilica an atrium with its cloisters and vestibules, which is not likely; and is, besides, contradicted by the title of the Chapter, which gives us the atrium in the singular number. Valesius conjectures that the *παρ' ἑκάτερα* should be transposed to the cloisters; *στοαί τ' ἐπὶ ταύτῃ παρ' ἑκάτερα.* It appears to me not impossible that we should read *ἦσαν δ' ἐξέδραι παρ' ἑκάτερα* for *ἦσαν δ' ἐνταυθοῖ παρ' ἑκάτερα*; for the *exedræ* are mentioned in the title, but not in the Chapter itself; and the words *ἐξέδραι* and *ἐνταυθοῖ* resemble each other sufficiently, especially when written in capitals, to be mistaken for each other. In the basilica at Tyre there were similarly *exedræ* and chambers on either side of the basilica, and connected with the front door,......*ἐξέδρας καὶ οἴκους τοὺς παρ' ἑκάτερα μεγίστους ἐπισκευάζων εὐτέχνως, ἐπὶ ταυτὸν εἰς πλευρὰ τῷ βασιλείῳ συνεζευγμένους, καὶ ταῖς ἐπὶ τὸν μέσον οἶκον εἰσβολαῖς ἡνωμένους.* (Eus. Eccl. Hist. lib. x. c. 4.) The *exedra* of the ancients appears to have been a recess or chamber, partly open, and provided with seats, often appended to a *porticus*; like the apses at the west end of Fig. 2. I have not attempted to delineate the *exedræ* of the entrance-court.

very middle of the wide market-place, stood the propylæa or vestibules of the whole work, which being decorated in the most imposing manner, afforded to those who were passing a promise of the wonders within.........This temple did the Emperor construct as a Martyrium of the Saving Resurrection, &c.

In the above description, after the Holy Sepulchre itself, we are introduced to a paved court, surrounded with porticoes, or cloisters on three of its sides, and having the Basilica on its fourth or eastern side. We are told that this side was opposite to the cave, by which, of course, is meant the entrance to the cave; for the history of the different states of the Holy Sepulchre in Section III. above, has shewn that it was an isolated edicula having its entrance to the East, and hence it must be inferred that the court here described surrounded the cave of the Sepulchre, and that the cloisters were opposite the sides and back of the monument, but that the Basilica occupied that side of the court which faced the entrance. I think it most probable that the cloisters were semicircular towards the West, following the present outline of the outer walls; for the excavation and levelling at this end seems to indicate such a form, and the outer wall of Constantine's cloister would be so far protected by the rock behind it, that it would probably escape obliteration. The rock shews at least that the court could not have extended farther West than the present building. In my restoration of the plan of the Basilica, (Fig. 2, Plate 1), I have delineated the cloistered court in this manner; and the positions of the North and South apses, which lie wholly to the west of the centre of the Rotunda, and opposite to the Sepulchre, seem to indicate that they were framed with reference to the semicircular form, and not to the circular form, which the Rotunda of after ages assumed. Thus it is not impossible that these apses were also parts of Constantine's cloister, for such semicircular recesses (or *exedræ*) are of frequent occurrence in Roman buildings[1]. But the restored plan which I have ventured to give must be considered as a mere diagram, shewing one out of many possible arrangements that may be conceived in coincidence with the description of Eusebius, which is far too loose, imperfect, and untechnical, to admit of certain interpretation into the accurate language of descriptive geometry. It may fairly be doubted, for example, whether the plural employed for the cloisters that surround the three sides of the court in question, is meant only for the three cloisters, one on each side, or is intended to convey the description of a double cloister on each side.

We now come to the Basilica; and to understand this it must be compared with those buildings of Constantine, the plan of which is better known to us. The whole of this Emperor's architectural works have been carefully collected and described by Ciampini[2]. The plans of his churches are of two kinds; the larger ones appear to have been in the form of a parallelogram with side aisles, as the Lateran, Vatican, and St Paul at Rome. Others were of a circular or polygonal form, but were intended either for baptisteries or mausolea; as the Baptistery of Constantine, and the Mausolea of his daughter Constantia, and his mother Helena, all at Rome.

---

[1] In the baths and temples at Rome, temples at Baiæ, Baalbec, Palmyra, palace of Diocletian at Spalatro, &c.

[2] J. Ciampini, de sacris Ædificiis a Constantino Magno constructis. (Romæ, 1693.)

At Constantinople he erected many which have disappeared; but it is remarkable that several of these are designated by the Byzantine historians as of a *dromical* form, a word singularly descriptive of a church with a rectangular body and an apse at the extremity; for the ancient *dromos*, or circus, was a parallelogram, square at one end, and circular at the other. St Sophia at Constantinople was, in its first state as Constantine built it, *dromical*, and so also were his churches of St Dynamis and St Agathonicus, in the same city. The great Church of the Apostles which he built for his burial-place was also *dromical*, and its sides were *cruciform*[1]. The church which he built at Antioch was octagonal.

There is nothing in the description of the Basilica, or House of Prayer, at the Holy Sepulchre, that would lead us to suppose its form to have been different from the parallelogram which I have just shewn to be the usual plan which the Emperor followed. It had double side-aisles, which we are told were partly above and partly below the ground. The survey of the original form of the ground, however, completely explains this phrase by shewing that to the present day the rock rises fifteen feet on the southern side of the site, and is exhibited on all sides, proving that the floor of the church must have been artificially sunk so much below the general surface, as to justify the expressions of our Author.

[1] M. Couchaud, in his treatise on the Eglises Byzantines de la Grèce, has fallen into the singular mistake of asserting that Eusebius tells us all Constantine's churches were erected on an octagonal or circular plan, and covered with a dome, (p. 2.) It is true that Eusebius tells us the church of Antioch was octagonal, (Lib. III. c. 50,) but that is the only one so described by him. The church of Paulinus at Tyre was a basilica, of the ordinary dromical form, with its entrance at the east end, as appears from the description given by Eusebius in the tenth book of his Ecclesiastical History.

The words which he uses, in telling us that the colonnades in front had great columns, and those within had square pedestals, have led some to suppose that the first sort were placed in front of the building *outside*, and the others inside. But I believe his meaning to be, that the columns occupied the front ranks within, and that there were smaller pillars on pedestals behind, separating the two side-aisles from each other. This was exactly the case with the ancient Basilica of St Peter at Rome, and I have accordingly so represented our Basilica in the restored Plan. No allusion is made to a transept by Eusebius, who merely tells us that the doors were at the east end of the church, and opposite to them, the apse. In placing a transept in my Plan I have therefore taken a gratuitous liberty, but have nevertheless followed strictly the precedent afforded me in the plans of the Roman basilicas of the Emperor; and I have done so because the arrangement of the ground with reference to the form of Calvary appeared to indicate a transept, of which more below. To turn the doors of a church to the east, and the apse to the west, although contrary to the subsequent practice of Christendom, was the more usual in the time of Constantine; St Peter's itself being so turned, and most others of that age. The obscurest part of the whole description is in the last chapter, which contains a huddled list of the architectural members about the entrance-court, which, after all, was probably nothing more than the usual cloistered court which I have shewn in the Plan[2].

[2] Fortunately there is no ambiguity in the conclusion of the Chapter, which tells us that the propylæum opened upon the market-place; a most valuable in-

The Portal, or general entrance to the "Martyrium of the Resurrection," as the whole group of buildings is termed by Eusebius, opened upon the market-place. Now the street which at present forms the eastern boundary, is occupied by deserted bazars, and the place, no doubt, has thus been devoted to merchandise from the time of Constantine. But at the very point where, in accordance with the explanation I have given above, the propylæum ought to be situated, there still exist the ruins of columns, which, as M. Schultz says, indicate the former presence of a Roman portal, of the original use of which however he does not appear to be aware. "If we pass through the deserted bazar," (at HL Fig. 1,) says he, (p. 60), "and beyond the southern end of it, we find three mutilated columns, which still remain erect, and project above the surface. A broken shaft of similar work lies on the ground. Behind the southernmost column, if we enter the neighbouring shops, we see in the one the lower part of a pilaster, and in the other the remains of a wall in the massive style of antiquity. These separate fragments correspond with each other, and suggest the conclusion that a great[1] portal stood here."

---

dication of the position of the Church, which completely oversets the opinions lately advanced by Mr Fergusson. This gentleman imagines that the golden gate in the eastern wall of the Temple area is no other than the propylæum in question, completely overlooking or neglecting this passage of Eusebius, which would compel him to fix the market-place in the Valley of Jehoshaphat; a location which, I need scarcely add, is ludicrously impossible.

[1] In Fig. 2. I have determined the probable dimensions of the basilica from comparison with those of the church at Bethlehem. This church was erected over the supposed place of the Nativity, at the same time as the Basilica of the Resurrection, and the Church of the Ascension. The Church of Bethlehem remains to this day, with its nave in plan so exactly corresponding to the age of Constantine, that we may be sure that it cannot have suffered essential altera-

In the Eusebian description just quoted, there is not only no allusion to the Cross discovered by Helena, but no mention of Golgotha or Calvary. The unity of purpose in the Martyrium which pervades his whole narrative is very remarkable. From the announcement of the Emperor's first intention to the full completion of the edifice, the one only object is to do honour and reverence to the Sepulchral Cave, and to that alone.

---

tion. Its transepts indeed appear too complex in plan for that period, and more resemble the works of Justinian, to whom the rebuilding of the Church is assigned by Eutychius. But, for an elaborate description of its history, I must refer my readers to the papers on the churches of Palestine in the Ecclesiologist of March and April, 1847, by the Author of the Holy City. A very good plan of the Church is given by Bernardino, but the usual difficulty of ascertaining the exact scale of measurement which he made use of, greatly diminishes its value. Fortunately the kindness of Charles Barry, Esq. has enabled me to present my readers with the English dimensions of the Church, which he measured and planned with his own hands. His plan agrees with Bernardino's. The interior dimensions are as follow :—

Measured East and West.

	ft.	in.
Width of narthex	19	9
Length of nave within walls	97	6
Width of transept, including thickness of west wall	33	7
Length of eastern limb of the Cross, exclusive of apse	30	7
Radius of apse	14	0
Total length from apse wall to western door	175	8

Measurements from North to South.

	ft.	in.
Length of narthex	50	2
Width of nave, central aisle	31	9
Total width of nave, including side-aisles	86	7
Total length of transept, from northern apse to southern apse inclusive	117	7

The nave has double side-aisles, and ten piers in the length, forming a colonnade of eleven intercolumns. The columns are of the Corinthian order: the height of their shafts about sixteen feet three inches, of the capitals one foot ten inches, of the architrave over them one foot three inches ; the diameter of the column is two feet one inch and a quarter ; and the height of the base and plinth thirteen inches and a quarter ; the plinth is two feet eleven inches square.

I found that the site of the present Church of the Sepulchre would admit a nave with double side-aisles of the same dimensions as that of Bethlehem, within a foot or two of the width, and accordingly I have so drawn it. It is evident that the side walls are limited on the south by the Rock of Calvary, and on the north apparently by the rock in which the "prison" is excavated ; also that the centre line of the

And the plan admirably provides for that purpose by furnishing a house of prayer close to it, and by enclosing the sacred spot itself in a court beyond the altar of the basilica.

The question that arises is, whether Calvary was altogether excluded and neglected, or whether it included itself, as a matter of course, from its known and scriptural proximity to the Holy Sepulchre. The only writer contemporary with Eusebius is the Bordeaux Pilgrim, and his visit to Jerusalem (A. D. 333) was made while the building was in progress, for it was begun in the year 326 and dedicated in 335. He says "that on the left hand is the little hill of Golgotha, where the Lord was crucified, and about a stone's throw from it the crypt wherein his body was laid, and whence on the third day he arose. There, at present, by command of the Emperor Constantine, a basilica is made, that is, a church of marvellous beauty, having at the side reservoirs whence water is drawn, and a bath behind where children are washed[1]."

---

entire building may be assumed to have passed through the Sepulchral Cavern, which was its main feature. The walls of the present choir, however, are not exactly directed eastwards; but the wall of the ancient corridor on the north appears, from Mr Scoles's plan, not to be parallel to the others, and to be nearer to a true easterly direction. I have inclined the axis of Constantine's Basilica so as to place it parallel to this line, and pass through the Portal in St Stephen Street. But my information on these relative positions is necessarily imperfect; and I hope that I may have succeeded in directing sufficient attention to these points to induce some future visitants to Jerusalem to examine them.

[1] "A sinistra autem parte est monticulus Golgotha, ubi Dominus crucifixus est. Inde quasi ad lapidem missum est crypta, ubi corpus ejus positum fuit et tertia die resurrexit. Ibidem modo jussu Constantini imperatoris basilica facta est; id est, Dominicum miræ pulchritudinis, habens ad latus exceptoria unde aqua levatur, et balneum à tergo, ubi infantes lavantur." (Itinerarium Hierosolymitanum, Vetera Romanorum Itineraria, Wesseling. Amst. 1735.)

We have here a cotemporary witness to the recognition of Golgotha, but no mention of the exact place or hole in which the Cross was planted[2].

St Cyril, also, who was ordained at Jerusalem by Macarius about 335, and became Bishop of Jerusalem in 350, has made in his lectures many allusions to the Golgotha, which are the more interesting because the lectures were delivered in the very Church we are considering, and contain repeated appeals to the places which surrounded the preacher and his congregation, as, for example, to "this holy Golgotha, rising on high and showing itself to this day, displaying even yet how because of Christ the rocks were then riven, the neighbouring sepulchre, where he was laid, and the stone which was laid on the door, which lies to this day by the tomb[3]." Other passages will be found in the note.

---

[2] Eusebius, in the Laudatory Oration for Constantine (c. 9), says that he, "at the place of the Lord's Martyrium, decorated with all kinds of magnificence a mighty house of prayer, and a sacred temple in honour of the Holy Cross; and he ornamented the monument of the Saviour with decorations that are indescribable." This seems to refer to a Chapel of the Crucifixion, in addition to the other buildings. We have no reason to suppose that Constantine intended to shew the same reverence for the site of the Crucifixion as for the Sepulchre.

[3] "The cleft (or entrance?) which was at the door of the Salutary Sepulchre...was hewn out of the rock itself, as it is customary here in the front of sepulchres. For now it appears not the outer cave having been hewn away for the sake of the present adornment; for before the sepulchre was decorated by royal zeal there was a cave in the face of the rock." (Cyril, Lect. XIV. 9.)

"This blessed Golgotha in which... we are now assembled." (IV. 10.)

"He who was crucified in this Golgotha." (IV. 14.)

"The Holy Ghost on the day of Pentecost descended on the Apostles... here in Jerusalem in the upper Church of the Apostles......And in truth it were most fitting that as we discourse concerning Christ and Golgotha upon this Golgotha, so also we should speak concerning the Holy Ghost in the upper Church." (XVI. 4.)

"Though I should deny (the Crucifixion), this Golgotha confutes me near which we are now assembled; the wood of the Cross confutes me which has from hence been distributed piecemeal to all the world." (XIII. 4.)

It is pretty clear from these expressions that if the exact seat of the Cross had not been fixed upon at this time, at least the site of Golgotha was supposed to be known, and apparently the rock rose up within the Church. It was in accordance with this hypothesis that I have ventured to introduce the transept and its southern chapel into the plan as one way in which this rock might have been displayed. The chapels, separated by a colonnade from the extremities of the transept, however, I have imitated from Constantine's

---

"For though it (the Sepulchre) be now adorned, and that most excellently, with royal gifts, yet it was before a garden, and the token and traces thereof remain." (XIV. 5.)

"The diligent chanters of the Church who imitate the angel-hosts, and continually sing praises to God, who are thought worthy to chant psalms in this Golgotha." (XIII. 26.)

"Wherefore is this place of Golgotha and of the Resurrection not called, like the other churches, a Church, but a Testimony? It was, perhaps, because of the Prophet, who had said (Zeph. iii. 8.) *On the day of my Resurrection at the testimony*." (XIV. 6.)

"The soldiers then surrendered the truth for silver, but the kings of this day have in their piety built this holy Church of the Resurrection of God our Saviour, inlaid with silver, and embossed with gold, in which we are assembled." (XIV. 14, 22, 23.)

"And after the holy and salutary day of Easter......ye shall come all the days of the following week after the assembly into the holy place of the Resurrection, and there ye shall hear other lectures." (XVIII. 33.)

This seems to shew, (according to Mr. Newman, from whose translation of the Catechetical Lectures I have selected the above passages,) that St. Cyril delivered his last five Lectures in the *Anastasis* or Church upon the site of the Holy Sepulchre; and Mr. Newman adds that St. Cyril delivered his first eighteen Lectures in the Basilica of Constantine or Church of the Holy Cross, (Euseb. Laud. c. 9) called also the *Martyrium* or Testimony, as being built close upon and in memory of our Lord's passion.

He has overlooked the passage which I have quoted immediately before this last, which proves that the fourteenth lecture was delivered in the *Anastasis*. There is therefore no reason to suppose that the last lectures were delivered in a different place from the first. According to my interpretation of the Eusebian descriptions there was no *church* upon the site of the Sepulchre, excepting the *edicula* of the Sepulchre which stood in the midst of an open court. Moreover, Eusebius winds up his account of the building by calling it "the *Martyrium of the Resurrection*," (L. 3. c. XL;) a name which appears to have been given to the whole building.

Basilica of St Peter at Rome, and have, therefore, cotemporary similarity to support them. It is not impossible that a representation of the Cross planted upon this Golgotha may have given rise to the improbable supposition of later ages, that the actual foot-hole of the Cross was known and preserved; for the first mention of this hole occurs so late as the seventh century, in the work of Arculfus, and he only tells us that a great silver Cross was planted on the very spot where the original Cross once stood at the Crucifixion.

The reservoirs of water mentioned by the Bordeaux Pilgrim, may be traced in several places. Some of them have already occurred to us. That called the Well of Helena, at the north-western corner, still supplies the inhabitants of the Church. The so-called "Prison" and the place of the "Invention of the Cross," are each described as resembling ancient cisterns; and, lastly, there is actually an enormous reservoir (at Z Fig. 3,) still in existence close to the north side of the Portal of Constantine in the street of St Stephen, which now bears the name of the Treasury of Helena, and which Schultz (p. 61) declares to be the most ancient and remarkable cistern which he had seen in Jerusalem. Mr. Williams informs me that he conjectures the dimensions to be at least sixty by thirty feet; but being full of water, and only to be viewed by torchlight from a platform on one side, it is very difficult to measure or even estimate its magnitude. It must be nearly upon a level with the excavation that is now occupied by the Chapel of St Helena.

This chapel in my plan of the Basilica falls partly within and partly without, as if a crypt had once stood on its site, so contrived as to be accessible from within the nave, and when once entered, to afford a passage under the atrium to the cavern where the Cross was discovered. The greater part of the sides of the chapel are certainly of rock, but I think it likely that an examination of the contiguous buildings on the north and east sides would show that similar excavations were originally extended in those directions, so as to connect this crypt with the cistern called the "Treasury of Helena."

There is no evidence to prove whether or no the cavern, at present shewn as the place of the Invention of the Cross, was the same in which that remarkable transaction took place. The historical evidence of the finding of the so-called three Crosses and Nails in the presence of St Helena and of Macarius, is so strong that it is impossible to doubt it. But it appears to me equally impossible to believe for an instant the genuineness of these relics, which, after all, were probably pieces of timber and iron-work belonging to foundations of some former structure, which, having been accidentally turned up in the course of the excavations, were promoted by the excited imagination of Helena to the high office which they immediately assumed. From the silence of Eusebius we may infer that he disbelieved their authenticity. However, they exercised so remarkable an influence upon the world, and especially upon church architecture, that their history is by no means to be lightly dismissed; for they were at once accepted by the Christian world as genuine, and venerated accordingly, to a degree which it is very difficult to believe or understand in our present state of feeling upon these subjects.

XI.

THE BUILDINGS OF THE SECOND PERIOD, FROM A.D. 614 TO A.D. 1010.

THE Martyrium of Constantine, described in the last chapter, was utterly ruined by the Persians in the year 614: the buildings were set fire to, and studiously demolished; and we shall find reason to believe that, in the re-building, the original plan was considerably altered: partly from the want of funds, and partly from the changes which had taken place in the forms and arrangements of churches, and from the additional *Holy Places* which had accumulated round about the Sepulchre by the growing traditions of the spot. At all events, the description of the Martyrium by Eusebius is exceedingly different from the description of the buildings on the spot during the second period. The history of this period[1] informs us that the credit of the restoration is principally due to Modestus, the Superior of the Monastery of Theodosius, who, as Eutychius in the tenth century, relates, "came to Jerusalem and constructed the Churches of the Resurrection, of the Sepulchre, of the Calvary, and of St Constantine, as they now exist[2]." The buildings on this spot had now, therefore, acquired the character of a group of three distinct churches, (the Sepulchre being included within the Church of the Resurrection); and these churches were not architecturally connected or symmetrically disposed, whereas, in the original Martyrium of Constantine, as I have shewn, the entire site was occupied by a symmetrical mass of building.

[1] Holy City, Vol. I. pp. 303, 4. [2] Eutychii Annales, Tom. II. p. 219.

The best and most satisfactory account of the plan of the Churches at this period is in the work of Adamnanus[1], which contains a most minute description, leaving scarcely anything to desire; and which, in its abbreviated form by Bede, was so entirely accepted during the early part of the middle ages, that the pilgrims commonly refer to it as an apology for not extending their own accounts. This description, however, was extracted by the diligent cross-questioning of Adamnanus, Abbot of Columba in Iona, from Arculfus the Pilgrim, who paid him a visit, and it was by the Abbot written down in the form in which it was presented to the world; he also induced Arculfus to draw him a rough plan of the churches upon a waxen tablet[2].

---

[1] Our principal authorities for the state of the buildings during this period are the above-cited Arculfus, (circa, A. D. 697,) Willibaldus, Bishop of Aicstadt, who was born at Southampton in the year 700, and made his pilgrimage in 765, the Pilgrim-monk Bernardus, A. D. 870; and Eutychius of Alexandria, who died in the year 940. The absurdly credulous Itinerary of Antoninus Placentinus appears to belong to the beginning of this period; but it is quite enough to say of this writer, that even the editors of the Acta Sanctorum are ashamed of the fables it contains, to which they apply the term "anile."

[2] This plan is wanting in the greater number of the manuscripts both of Adamnanus and of the abridgement by Bede. In fact, I believe the copy of it which is to be found in Mabillon, (Acta Sanctorum, Ord. S. Ben[t]. Sæc. 3. Part II. p. 504) Adamnanus, and also in Quaresmius, is derived from Gretser's edition of Adamnanus, and he tells us that he took it from a Belgian manuscript. Gretser's text has been corrected by Mabillon from other and better manuscripts; but his copy of the diagram differs only from Gretser's in being more neatly drawn and with some differences of proportion; while Gretser's has much more the air of a fac-simile of the original. This original has probably suffered much distortion, from being the result of a series of copies from one manuscript to another; but it has a singular resemblance to the actual site when due allowance is made for the rough method of drawing, and the total want of scale. This Plan has been published so often, that I have not thought it worth while to reproduce it. Copies of it are engraved in the following works :—Quar-

I shall now proceed to extract and translate from the tract of Adamnanus all that belongs to the churches on this site, omitting only his description of the Sepulchre itself, which I have already given in a previous section.

" *Of the Church of the Sepulchre of the Lord.*

" Concerning these things we diligently interrogated the holy Arculfus, and especially about the Sepulchre of the Lord, and the Church constructed above it, of which he delineated the form for me upon a waxen tablet. This great Church, all of stone, of wondrous rotundity on all sides, arising from its foundation in three walls, has a broad passage between each wall and the next. In three ingeniously constructed places of the middle wall three altars are disposed, one looking to the South, another to the North, and the third towards the West; and this round and lofty Church is sustained by twelve columns of wondrous magnitude, and it has eight doors or entrances formed by three walls erected in the intermediate spaces between the passages. Of these, four are turned to the South-East, and the other four to the North-East." Here follows the description of the Sepulchre already given in Section VII. above. And he then proceeds to say that there are " some things to be said concerning the buildings of the other sacred places."

terly Review, March, 1845, p. 355. Fergusson's Jerusalem, p. 149. Quaresmius, T. II. p. 585. Acta Sanctorum, Ord[s]. S. Ben[i]. Sæc. III. p. 505. Gretseri Op. Ratis. 1734. T. IV. p. 256. Lastly, Dr. Giles has given one which differs from this, in his edition of Bede, Vol. VI. p. 439. He found it in a manuscript in the Royal Library at Paris, No. 2321.

" *Of the Church of St Mary.*

The quadrangular Church of Holy Mary, the Mother of the Lord, is joined on the right side to that round Church described above, and which is called Anastasis or Resurrection, because it is constructed on the place of the Lord's Resurrection.

" *Of the Church of Calvary.*

" Another Church, of great magnitude (N)[1], is constructed towards the East in that place which is called Golgotha. In its upper parts there hangs by ropes a certain brazen *rota* with lamps, beneath which a great silver cross is infixed in the very same place where formerly the wooden cross, on which the Saviour of mankind suffered, was fixed and stood.

" *Note.*

" In the same Church there is a cave cut out of the rock beneath the place of the Lord's Cross, where the sacrifice is offered upon an altar for the souls of certain honoured persons, whose bodies meanwhile, lying in the street, are placed before the door (*f*) of the said Golgothan Church, until the holy mysteries for the defunct are finished.

" *Of the Basilica of Constantine.*

" To this Church, constructed on a quadrangular plan in the place of Calvary, there adjoins on the Eastern side that neighbouring stone Basilica (W), erected with great magnificence by the royal Constantine, called also the Martyrium, which was located, as they say, in the place where the cross of our Lord, with the other two crosses

[1] This and the following letters of reference belong to Fig. 3, Plate 1.

of the thieves, concealed under the earth, was found by the gift of the Lord, after two hundred and thirty-three years. Between these two Churches occurs that famous place (*g*) where Abraham the Patriarch erected an altar for the sacrifice of Isaac.........where now there stands a small wooden table upon which people offer alms for the poor .... Between the 'Anastasis,' that is, the above-described Church, and the Basilica of Constantine is a small court (S) extending as far as the Golgothan Church, in which court lamps are kept constantly burning day and night.

"*Of the other Exedra in the Church of Calvary.*

"Between the Golgothan Church and the Martyrium is a certain 'Exedra,' or apse (P), in which is the Cup." This Arculfus goes on to describe as the Cup of the Last Supper, and also to state that he saw the "sponge" and the "lance[2]."

---

[2] I subjoin the original text of Adamnanus from Mabillon (Acta Sanctorum, Sæc. III. p. 2, 504), which he derived from the Vatican and Corbeian Manuscripts and from Gretser's edition which is published in his Works. Ratisbon, 1734. T. IV. p. 254.

"*De Ecclesia Sepulcri Domini.*

"De quibus diligentiùs interrogavimus sanctum Arculfum, præcipuè de Sepulchro Domini, et Ecclesia super illud constructa, cujus mihi formam in tabula cerata ipse depinxit. Quæ utique grandis Ecclesia tota lapidea, mira rotunditate ex omni parte collocata à fundamentis in tribus consurgens parietibus, inter unumquemque parietem et alterum, latum habens spatium viæ; tria quoque altaria in tribus locis parietis medii artificè fabricatis. Hanc rotundam et summam Ecclesiam suprà memorata habentem altaria, unum ad Meridiem respiciens, alterum ad Aquilonem, tertium versus Occasum, duodecim miræ magnitudinis lapideæ sustentant columnæ. Hæc bis quaternales portas habet, hoc est, introitus, per tres è regione interjectis viarum spatiis stabilitos parietes: ex quibus quatuor exitus ad Vulturnum spectant, qui et Calcius dicitur ventus; alii vero quatuor ad Eurum respiciunt."......

Here follows the description of the "Tegurium" and Holy Sepulchre already given above in Section VII.

Thus we have a group of four churches, (1) the Anastasis; (2) the Church or Chapel of St Mary; (3) the Golgothan Church; and (4) the Basilica of Constantine. But the Church of St Mary appears to have been small and insignificant, for it is mentioned with no epithet of praise, either for magnificence or mag-

---

"*Nota**.

"In eadem verò Ecclesia quædam in petra habetur excisa spelunca, infrà locum Dominicæ Crucis, ubi super altare pro quorundam honoratorum animabus sacrificium offertur, quorum corpora interim in platea jacentia, ponuntur ante januam ejusdem Golgothanæ Ecclesiæ, usque quo finiantur illa pro ipsis defunctis sacrosancta mysteria. Has itaque quaternalium figuras Ecclesiarum, juxta exemplar, quod mihi ut superius dictum est, S. Arculphus in paginula figuravit cerata, depinximus, non quod possit eorum similitudo formari in pictura, sed ut Dominicum monumentum tali, licèt vili figuratione; in medietate rotundæ Ecclesiæ constitutum monstretur et quæ huic propior Ecclesia vel quæ eminus est posita declaretur.

"*De Ecclesia B. Mariæ.*

"Cæterum de sanctorum structuris locorum pauca addenda sunt aliqua. Illi rotundæ Ecclesiæ suprà sæpius memoratæ, quæ et *Anastasis*, hoc est, Resurrectio vocitatur, eò quòd in loco Dominicæ Resurrectionis fabricata est; à dextra cohæret parte sanctæ Mariæ Matris Domini quadrangulata Ecclesia.

"*De Ecclesia Calvariæ.*

"Alia verò prægrandis Ecclesia Orientem versùs in illo fabricata est loco, qui Hebraicè Golgotha vocitatur, cujus in superioribus grandis quædam ærea cum lampadibus rota in funibus pendet, infra† quam magna argentea crux infixa statuta est eodem in loco ubi quondam lignea crux, in qua passus est humani generis Salvator, infixa stetit.

"*De Basilica Constantini.*

"Huic Ecclesiæ in loco Calvariæ quadrangulata fabricatæ structura, lapidea illa vicina Orientali in parte cohæret Basilica, magno cultu, a Rege Constantino constructa, quæ et Martyrium appellatur; in eo, ut fertur, fabricata loco, ubi Crux Domini, cum aliis latronum binis crucibus sub terra abscondita, post ducentorum triginta trium cyclos annorum, ipso Domino donante, reperta est.

"Inter has itaque duales Ecclesias ille famosus occurrit locus, in quo Abraham Patriarcha altare composuit, super

* The "*Nota*" is evidently intended to follow the chapter "*De Ecclesia Calvariæ*," or the conclusion of the whole description, and I have accordingly transposed it in the translation.

† This concluding sentence, "infra...stetit," is in Gretser's copy placed at the end of the preceding article, and thus applied to the Church of St. Mary. I follow Mabillon's text, which also agrees with Bede's abridgement.

nitude as the others are[1]. It is not alluded to by Antoninus Placentinus, or by Eutychius, who only speaks of three Churches whenever he has occasion to refer to this group: namely, the Resurrection, the Calvary, and St Constantine[2].

---

illud imponens lignorum struem; et, ut Isaac immolaret filium suum, evaginatum arripuit gladium; ubi nunc mensa habetur lignea non parva, super quam pauperum eleemosynæ à populo offeruntur......Inter Anastasim, hoc est, Ecclesiam suprà memoratam et Basilicam Constantini quædam patet plateola, usque ad Ecclesiam Golgothanam, in qua plateola die ac nocte semper lampades ardent.

"*De alia Exedra in Ecclesia Calvariæ.*

"Inter illam quoque Golgothanam Ecclesiam et Martyrium quædam inest Exedra in qua est calix Domini, quem à se benedictum propria manu in cœna pridie quàm pateretur, ipse conviva Apostolis tradidit convivantibus. Qui argenteus calix sextarii Gallici mensuram habet duasque ansulas in se ex utraque parte altrinsecus continet compositas. In quo utique calice inest spongia, quam aceto plenam hyssopo circumponentes Dominum crucifigentes obtulerunt ori ejus. De hoc eodem calice, ut fertur, Dominus post Resurrectionem cum Apostolis convivans bibit. Quem S. Arculfus vidit, et illius scrinioli ubi reconditus habetur operculi foramen pertusi manu tetigit propria osculatus........

"*De lancea militis.*

"Et illam conspexit lanceam militis, quâ lancea latus Domini in Cruce pendentis ipse percusserat. Hæc eadem lancea, in porticu illius Constantini Basilicæ inserta habetur in cruce lignea cujus hastile in duas intercisum est partes.

[1] It seems to be the same which Sæwulf afterwards placed over the stone of Unction, and which W. of Tyre mentions as a small oratory. If so, it may have been at M in the plan. Or perhaps it was nearer to the campanile, as the stone would be considered as a moveable relic.

[2] Eutychii Ann. pp. 212, 219, 243. The earliest testimony of this period of the buildings is given by Antiochus the monk, who lived about 630, in the time of Heraclius. Describing the buildings of Modestus, he mentions *three* churches in this spot. "Modestus....templa Salvatoris nostri Jesu Christi, quæ quidem barbarico igne conflagrarunt, in sublime erigit omni prorsus digna veneratione, puta *ædes sanctæ Calvariæ ac sanctæ Resurrectionis; domum insuper dignam omni honore venerandæ Crucis*, quæ mater Ecclesiarum est." Ant. Mon. Epist. ad Eustachium Mag. Bib. Patr. Par. 1644. Tom. xii. p. 10.

Willibaldus, A.D. 765:—"venit ad Hierusalem in illum locum ubi inventa fuerat S^a^ Crux Domini. Ibi nunc est Ecclesia in illo loco qui dicitur Calvariæ locus, et hæc fuit prius extra Hierusalem. Sed beata Helena quando invenit, collocavit illum locum intus intra Hierusalem. Et ibi stant tres

Bernardus describes the group as of "four churches connected together by walls, that is to say, one to the East which has Mount Calvary; and (*one in*) the place in which the Cross of the Lord was found, which is called the Basilica of Constantine; another to the South, and a *fourth* to the West, in the middle of which is the Sepulchre of the Lord."........."Between these four Churches is a *Paradise* without a roof, the walls of which shine with gold, and the pavement with precious marble. In the midst of it is an enclosure of four chains, which proceed from the aforesaid four Churches, and in it is said to be the center of the world[1]." This enumeration of four churches agrees with that of Arculfus, if we

---

cruces ligneæ foris in Orientali plaga Ecclesiæ secus parietem, ad memoriam sanctæ Crucis Dominicæ et aliorum qui cum eo crucifixi erant.

"Illæ non sunt intus in Ecclesia, sed foris stant sub tecto extra Ecclesiam. Et ibi secus est ille hortus, in quo fuit Sepulchrum Salvatoris." Acta Sanctorum, Ord. S. Ben., Sæc. 3.

[1] "Intra hanc civitatem (Hierusalem,) exceptis aliis ecclesiis, quatuor eminent ecclesiæ, mutuis sibimet parietibus cohærentes: una videlicet ad Orientem quæ habet montem Calvariæ, et locum in quo reperta fuit Crux Domini et vocatur Basilica Constantini; alia ad Meridiem, *tertia** ad Occidentem, in cujus medio est Sepulchrum Domini, habens ix. columpnas in circuitu sui, inter quas consistunt parietes ex optimis lapidibus; ex quibus ix. columpnis, iv. sunt ante faciem ipsius monumenti, quæ cum suis parietibus claudunt lapidem coram sepulcro positum, quem Angelus revolvit, et super quem sedit post perpetratam Domini resurrectionem. De hoc sepulcro non est necesse plura scribere, cùm dicat Beda in historia sua inde sufficientia, quæ et nos possumus referre......Inter prædictas igitur iv. ecclesias est *Paradisus* sine tecto cujus parietes auro radiant; pavimentum verò lapide struitur pretiosissimo, habens in medio sui confinium iv. catenarum, quæ veniunt à prædictis quatuor ecclesiis, in quo dicitur medius esse mundus." Acta Sanctorum, Ord[s]. S. Ben. Tom. III. p. 2; also Recueil de Voyages, Tom. IV. p. 789. Par. 1839.

* I have substituted *fourth* for *tertia* in translating this passage, as the readiest mode of correcting the evident obscurity of it; for as it stands, four churches are mentioned and only three described; but there are other obvious symptoms of careless transcription in it which are not worth discussion.

suppose his southern church to be the Church of St Mary.

The description which is given by Arculfus of the construction of the Round Church and its entrances is very obscure and strange. Of its three walls it appears certain that the middle one was, properly speaking, the external wall, for it contained the apses that still exist for the altars; and the outer wall of his description was probably an external peristyle or cloister, as in the Church of St Fosca at Torcello[2].

In the Plan[3] (Fig. 3, Plate 1) I have dotted a circular wall (*a b c d*) in the probable position of this peristyle, and I have carried it concentrically round the Western end of the Church (*b c d*), for the mere purpose of shewing that the rising ground and rock at the West makes it very improbable that the circuit was so carried round at this end. Arculfus is but a loose describer, or rather, perhaps, his interpreter and amanuensis, Adamnanus, was not successful in extracting his meaning; and, after all, his work was merely the result of recollections, recalled to oblige the Abbot after his return from the pilgrimage. His description of St Sophia at Constantinople may shew how far his usual expressions are to be literally understood; for he actually uses the same words as in his account of the Round Church of the Anastasis. He says it is a "triple

[2] Vide Agincourt, pl. 26, Gally Knight. Ecc. Arch. of Italy, pl. 29. v. 1. The round church or mausoleum of Constantia at Rome had also an exterior peristyle. (Ciampini, de Sac. Æd. p. 135.)

[3] This plan is drawn from the account of Sæwulf, to illustrate the state of the churches in the subsequent period. But that state differed so little from the churches of Arculfus, that, by the help of a few dotted lines, I have made it also subservient to the illustration of the second period, which we are now considering. The long range of chapels, A, B, C, I, are the principal points of difference between the two.

stone church, rising from its foundations in three walls," upon which the dome rests, and that there is "between each of the above walls a broad space[1]," &c.

By the outer space in this case he must mean the first narthex or vestibule of St Sophia, which extends only along the front. But the whole phraseology of this sentence is sufficient to shew how large a licence we may assume in explaining his descriptions. I presume, therefore, that the outer passage in the Church of the Anastasis was confined to the Eastern half of the rotunda. His entrances to the North-east and South-east would differ but little in position from those of the subsequent Church, as shewn in the plan at D and H. The nature of the ground forbad a convenient entrance to the West, and the reverence due to the Sepulchre seems to have equally hindered a central Eastern Entrance. Indeed, an altar was placed opposite to the door of the Sepulchre at F, as Arculfus relates. The pilgrims were therefore naturally admitted at the South-west (at D), so that they might pass across in front of the Sepulchre, and after visiting it be dismissed in a similar manner at the North-east door (at H), to visit the other "holy places." But the quadruple construction of these entrances is very difficult to understand. Perhaps by the three walls we must understand three piers; and thus we get a group of four arches in the outer wall of the peristyle; and the middle wall might only have had a single

[1] "Cæterum de celeberrima ejusdem civitatis rotunda miræ magnitudinis lapidea Ecclesia,......quæ ab imo fundamentorum in tribus consurgens parietibus triplex, supra illos altiùs sublimata, rotundissima et nimis pulchra, simplici consummatur culminata camera. Hæc arcubus suffulta grandibus, inter singulos supra memoratos parietes latum habet spatium, vel ad inhabit andum, vel ad exorandum Deum, aptum et commodum." L. III. c. 3. p. 275.

doorway, as usual. What he calls the inner wall is, of course, the circle of columns as at present; but Arculfus mentions twelve columns. I presume that in fact the Eastern apse F, which is shewn in Fig. 3, did not exist in the buildings of Modestus. If the plan of the columns be completed in the eastern half, in the same manner as it stands in the western, we obtain twelve *columns* divided into four groups by four pair of *square piers;* which is a probable arrangement; for twelve columns alone would scarcely have been sufficient to carry the wall. The present three western apses (J, K, L) are, in all probability, upon the same foundations as the old ones[2].

The Golgothan Church is described as a very large one, and can scarcely, therefore, have occupied less ground than I have assigned to it at N in the outline, where it appears with three aisles. The cavern in the rock under the place of the Cross was, of course, the present apse of the Chapel of Adam, and the other exedra or apse, where the relics were kept, may have been placed at P, as I have indicated it. This Church was not rebuilt after Hakem destroyed the whole, for the Crusaders found only a small oratory over the place of the Crucifixion. Probably some remains of it are worked up into the present chapels, and may account for their irregularity of plan[3].

---

[2] It may be supposed, on the other hand, that the inner circle of this church was smaller than the present one, and that the outer circle was of the same diameter; but I do not think this so probable as the explanation I have given above.

[3] To complete the authorities I subjoin the account which Antoninus Placentinus gives of these buildings.

"A monumento usque Golgotha sunt gressus LXXX. Ab una parte ascenditur per gradus, unde Dominus ascendit ad crucifigendum. Nam in

The so-called Basilica of Constantine was perhaps the existing Chapel of S. Helena (W); for I have shewn its similarity to the Byzantine churches; and as Sæwulf and others who describe this spot between Hakem's destruction and the Crusaders' works, speak of this Church as in ruins, it must have been erected during this second period.

---

loco ubi fuit crucifixus, apparet cruor sanguinis. Et in ipso latere petræ est altare Patriarchæ Abraham, in quo ibat offerre Isaac, quando tentavit eum Dominus. Ibi et Melchisedech obtulit sacrificium Abrahæ quando revertabatur cum victoria à cæde Amelech, tunc ibidem dedit ei Abraham omnem decimationem in hostias. Juxta ipsum altare est crypta, ubi ponis aurem et audis flumina aquarum, et jactas pomum aut aliud quod natare potest, et vadis ad Siloa fontem ubi illud recipies. Intra Siloa et Golgotha credo est milliarium: nam Hierosolyma aquam vivam non habet, præter in Siloa fonte.

"De Golgotha usque ubi inventa est Crux sunt gressus L. In Basilica Constantini cohærente circa monumentum vel Golgotha, in atrio ipsius Basilicæ, est cubiculum ubi lignum Crucis reconditum est, quam adoravimus et osculavimus. Nam et titulum, qui super caput ejus positus fuerat, in quo scriptum est 'Jesus Nazarenus Rex Judæorum,' tenui in manu et osculatus sum. Lignum Crucis de nuce est: procedente vero sancta Cruce de cubiculo suo apparet stella in cœlo et venit super locum ubi Crux residet, et dum adoratur Crux stat super eam stella et ad fertur oleum ad benedicendum ampullis onychinis: hora vero qua tetigerit lignum Crucis ampullas mox ebullit foras. Revertente Cruce in locum suum et stella pariter revertitur, et post reclusam Crucem non apparet stella. Etiam ibi est Canna et Spongia de quibus legitur in Evangelio, cum qua Spongia aquam bibimus, et Calix onychinus quem benedixit Dominus in cœna, e aliæ multæ virtutes: Species B. Mariæ in superiori loco, et zona ipsius, et ligamentum quo in capite utebatur: et ibi sunt septem cathedræ marmoreæ seniorum." (Antonini Placentini Itinerarium. Acta Sanctorum, Maii. Tom. II. p. 10.)

The distances given in this passage are the only things worth attending to "From the Sepulchre to Golgotha LXXX. gressus," "from Golgotha to the place where the Cross was found, L. gressus." Measuring upon Mr. Scoles' accurate plan of the church, I find the distance from the middle of the altar of the Sepulchre to the foot-hole of the Cross to be 143 English feet; and the distance from the said foot-hole to the centre of the apse in the chapel of the Invention, by a singular coincidence to be also 143 English feet.

Gressus is the traveller's step (varying with the individual,) and not an established measure of length, like

XII.

THE BUILDINGS OF THE THIRD PERIOD, FROM A.D. 1010 TO A.D. 1099.

The third period exhibits to us the restoration of the buildings after their malicious and systematic destruction by the fanatic Caliph Hakem, in the year 1010[1]. This restoration seems to have been commenced or attempted almost immediately afterwards by Hakem or his mother, but was not effectually undertaken for several years, when the emperors of Constantinople, Romanus Argyrus, Michael the Paphlagonian, and Constantine Monomachus, in succession opened and concluded the necessary negotiations, and furnished the funds and architects, by which means the buildings were completed in A.D. 1048, or, at least, brought to the state in which the Crusaders found them. The best description of this state of the churches is given by the traveller Sæwulf, who performed his pilgrimage in the years 1102 and 1103, and whose account is contained in a manuscript preserved at Corpus Christi College,

---

the *passus*. "Memorandum quod 24 steppys sive gressus mei faciunt 12 virgas," quoth William Wyrcester: Nasmith. p. 83. It must be presumed, that LXXX. is a transcriber's error for XXXX.; and 40 paces for one, with 50 paces for the other distance, are not very far from the truth, especially as we do not know the exact points between which the distance was measured. Mr. Fergusson, (p. 126,) confounds the "gressus" with the "passus," and contrives to interpret this author so as to give 400 feet between the Sepulchre and Golgotha. Distances written numerically are never to be depended upon in manuscripts.

[1] Vide Part I. p. 352 above, for the detailed history of these events. The Emperor Romanus died in 1034; Michael, his successor, in 1041; and Constantine, who succeeded to the throne in 1042, reigned until 1054.

Cambridge[1]. As he arrived at the Holy City only two years after the Crusaders' conquest of Jerusalem, he saw and described the spot before the operations of enlargement and restoration, which they undertook so magnificently. It will be necessary, therefore, to give a translation of his entire description. I have constructed the plan, Fig. 3, by comparing this description with the buildings that exist; from which, as I have already shewn, there is little or no difficulty in picking out the portions that were standing before the Crusaders' works were added.

"The entrance of the city of Jerusalem is to the West, under the tower of David the king, by a gate which is called David's Gate. The first place to visit is the Church of the Holy Sepulchre, not only on account of the arrangement of the streets, but also because of its great renown above all other churches......In the midst of this Church is the Lord's Sepulchre, girt about with a very strong wall, and covered over to prevent the rain from falling upon the sacred Sepulchre, because the church overhead is left open......In the court of the Church of the Holy Sepulchre several holy places are to be seen, to wit, *the Prison* (V), in which, according to the Assyrian tradition, our Lord was incarcerated after he was delivered up. A little above this is *the place* (X) *where the Holy Cross, with the other crosses, was found*, and where, subsequently, a large Church (W) was

[1] MSS. Corpus Christi Coll. Camb. No. III. 8. Nasmith's Catalogue, pp. 119, 120. This narrative was printed by Michel from Mr. Wright's transcript in the fourth Volume of the Recueil de Voyages par la Société de Geographie, Paris, 1839; but this transcript appear to have been hastily made, and although generally correct, has some omissions. I have collated and corrected the portion relating to this church with the original.

built in honour of Queen Helena, but afterwards utterly destroyed by the Pagans; below this, and not far from the prison, is seen a *marble Column*, to which our Lord was bound in the pretorium, and sorely scourged. Close to this is the *place where He was stripped* of His clothing by the soldiers; and next, the *place where He was clad* in a purple robe and crowned with thorns, and they divided His garments and cast lots.

"After this *Mount Calvary* (N) is ascended, where Abraham the Patriarch, having made an altar (*g*), would have sacrificed his only son in obedience to the Divine command; and where, afterwards, the Son of God, whom he prefigured, was sacrificed for the redemption of the world. The rock itself of the mountain bears witness to the Passion, being much split close to the pit in which the Cross was planted, as it is written, 'the rocks were rent.' Below is the place which is called Golgotha (N), where Adam is said to have been raised from the dead[2]......Close to Calvary, *the Church of S. Mary* (M) stands in the place where the Lord's Body, taken down from the Cross, was wrapped in linen with spices before it was buried.

"At the head of the Church of the Sepulchre, in the outer wall, not far from Calvary, is the place called *Compas* (*a*), where the Lord indicated with his own hand the centre of the world, as the Psalmist witnesses, 'For God is my King of old, working salvation in the midst of the earth[3].' But some say that it was here that He appeared to Mary Magdalen when she took Him to be the gardener.

---

[2] See Sect. VIII. above.

[3] Ps. lxxiii. 12. Vide Sect. VIII. above.

" These most holy oratories are situated in the court of the Sepulchre on the eastern part. But two Chapels (I, C), in honour of S. Mary and S. John, adhere to the very sides of the Church, one on each hand, even as these witnesses of the Passion stood one on each side of the Cross. On the western wall of the Chapel of S. Mary is to be seen painted on the outside a figure of the Virgin, by which Mary of Egypt......was marvellously consoled, as her life relates.

" On the other side of the Church of S. John is the beautiful Church of the Holy Trinity (B), in which is the place of baptism: to this adheres the Chapel of S. James (A), the apostle who first obtained the pontifical chair of Jerusalem. And these are so arranged, that any one standing in the last Church can see all the five churches from door to door.

" Beyond the gate of the Church of the Holy Sepulchre to the South, is the Church of S. Mary, which is called *Latina*, because there Monks perform the Latin service, and the Syrians say that the Virgin stood during the Crucifixion on the very spot where the altar of that Church is fixed.

" To this Church adheres the Church of S. Mary the Less, where nuns serve the Virgin and her Son; and close to this stands the Hospital where the celebrated Church or Monastery is dedicated in honour of S. John Baptist[1]."

---

[1] Relatio de Peregrinatione Sæwulfi ad Hierosolymam et Terram Sanctam. Annis Dominicæ Incarnationis 1102 et 1103. p. 83.

"Introitus civitatis Jerosolimam est ad Occidentem, sub arce David regis per portam quæ vocatur porta David. Primum eundem est ad Ecclesiam Sancti Sepulcri quæ Martyrium vocatur, non solum pro conditione platearum, sed quià celebrior est omnibus aliis ecclesiis.........In medio autem

The most curious part of this description is that which relates to the series of chapels annexed to the Round Church, and which I have already explained in Section VIII. I shall therefore merely refer to the Plan, Fig. 3, and to that explanation. These were apparently

---

istius Ecclesiæ est Dominicum Sepulchrum muro fortissimo circumcinctum et opertum, ne dùm pluit, pluvia cadere possit super Sanctum Sepulchrum, quià Ecclesia desuper patet discooperta. Ista Ecclesia sita est in declivio montis Syon sicut civitas.........

"In atrio Ecclesiæ Dominici Sepulchri loca visuntur sanctissima, scilicet carcer ubi Dominus noster Jesus Christus post traditionem incarceratus fuit, testantibus Assiriis; deinde paulo superiùs locus apparet ubi sancta Crux cum aliis crucibus inventa est, ubi posteà in honore reginæ Helenæ magna constructa fuit ecclesia, sed postmodum a paganis funditùs est detrusa; inferius vero non longè a carcere columpna marmorea conspicitur ad quam Jesus Christus Dominus noster in pretorio ligatus flagris affligebatur durissimis; juxta est locus ubi Dominus Noster a militibus exuebatur ab indumentis; deinde est locus ubi induebatur veste purpureâ a militibus et coronabatur spineâ coronâ, et diviserunt vestimenta sua sortem mittentes.

"Postea ascenditur in montem Calvarium, ubi Abraham patriarcha, facto altari, prius filium suum jubente Deo sibi immolare voluit, ibidem posteà Filius Dei, quem ipse prefiguravit, pro redemptione mundi Deo Patri immolatus est hostia; scopulus autem ejusdem montis Passionis Dominicæ testis juxtà fossam in quâ Dominica Crux fuit affixa multùm scissus, quià sinè scissura necem Fabricatoris sufferre nequivit sicut in Passione legitur, 'et petræ scissæ sunt.' Subtùs est locus qui Golgotha vocatur, ubi Adam a torrente Dominici cruoris super eum delapso dicitur esse a mortuis resuscitatus, sicut in Domini Passione legitur, 'et multa corpora sanctorum qui dormierant surrexerunt.' Sed in sententiis beati Augustini legitur eum sepultum fuisse in Hebron, ubi etiam postmodum tres patriarchæ sepulti sunt cum uxoribus suis, Abraham cum Sarâ, Isaac cum Rebeccâ, Jacob cum Liâ; et ossa Joseph, quæ filii Israel adportaverunt secum de Egypto. Juxtà locum Calvariæ, Ecclesia sanctæ Mariæ in loco ubi Corpus Dominicum, avulsum a cruce antequam sepeliretur, fuit aromatisatum et linteo sive sudario involutum.

"Ad caput autem Ecclesiæ Sancti Sepulchri, in muro forinsecùs non longè a loco Calvariæ, est locus qui Compas vocatur, ubi ipse Dominus noster Jesus Christus medium mundi propriâ manu, esse signavit atque mensuravit, psalmistâ testante, "Dominus autem Rex noster antè secula; operatus est salutem in medio terræ;" sed quidam in illo loco Dominum Jesum Christum dicunt apparuisse primo Mariæ Magdalenæ, dùm ipsa flendo eum quæsivit et putavit eum hortulanum fuisse, sicut Evangelista narrat.

"Ista oratoria sanctissima continentur in atrio Dominici Sepulchri ad Orien-

the buildings upon which the Greek Emperors expended their pains and funds. For the other holy places appear to have been merely protected by small oratories, according to the description of William of Tyre already quoted. The Prison was probably then in the same state as it is now, a dry vaulted cistern in the rock.

Of the place where the Cross was found, the same may be said. The Church or Chapel of S. Helena seems to have been in ruins, for Sæwulf speaks of it as in this state; and the anonymous historian, whose Tract is printed in the "Gesta Dei," and who also writes at the same period, says of this spot, "Near the Sepulchre, a little on one side, there rises a rock, split and gaping open, as it is written "that the rocks were rent," and beneath it is Golgotha.........A little further

---

talem plagam. In lateribus vero ipsius ecclesiæ *duæ* capellæ sibi adherent præclarissimæ hinc inde, *Scæ. Marie scilicet Scique Johannis in honore**, sicut ipsi participes Dominicæ Passionis sibi in lateribus constiterunt hinc inde.

"In muro autem Occidentali ipsius capellæ Sanctæ Mariæ conspicitur imago ipsius Domini genitricis perpicta exterius, quæ Mariam Egyptiacam olim toto corde compunctam atque ipsius Dei genitricis juvamen efflagitantem in figura ipsius cujus pictura erat, per Spiritum Sanctum loquendo mirifice consolabatur sicut in vita ipsius legitur.

"Ex alterâ vero parte Sancti Johannis ecclesiæ est monasterium Sanctæ Trinitatis pulcherrimum, in quo est locus baptisterii, cui adheret capella Sancti Jacobi apostoli, qui primam cathedram pontificalem Jerosolimis obtinuit; ita compositæ et ordinatæ omnes, ut quilibet in ultimâ stans ecclesiâ omnes quinque ecclesias perspicere potest clarissimè per ostium ad ostium.

"Extrâ portam Ecclesiæ Sancti Sepulchri ad Meridiem est Ecclesia Sanctæ Mariæ, quæ Latina vocatur, eò quod Latinè ibi Domino a monachis semper ministrabatur, et Assirii dicunt ipsam beatam Dei genitricem in crucifixione Filii sui Domini nostri stare in eodem loco ubi altare est ejusdem ecclesiæ. Cui ecclesiæ alia adheret Ecclesia Sanctæ Mariæ, quæ vocatur Parva, ubi monachæ conversantur sibi Filioque suo servientes devotissimè. Juxta quam est hospitale ubi monasterium habetur præclarum in honore Sancti Johannis Baptistæ dedicatum."

* The passages in Italics are omitted in the French transcript.

is the place called of 'Calvary,' where the wood of the Cross was found by Helena the blessed...and where was founded by the same Queen a Church of wondrous magnitude and workmanship, afterwards destroyed by perfidious Gentiles. The ruins which exist there attest the quality of the work[1]."

I have already stated my opinion, that the ruins alluded to by Sæwulf and this anonymous writer, are those of the present chapel, which was merely restored and revaulted by the Crusaders. Expressions of magnitude must always be taken with caution, for all ancient writers exaggerate in this respect; and we have seen that the plan of the actual Basilica of Constantine was very different from that of the chapel in question which bore its name in the Middle Ages.

The Column of Flagellation, and the other places which follow in Sæwulf's narrative, were probably in the open air; and even Calvary itself has no chapel given to it by Sæwulf; but it is the first of the three oratories mentioned by William of Tyre, of which the second is the place where the Cross was found, and the third is the place of Anointing, which Sæwulf describes as the church or chapel of S. Mary. On the whole, however, the general plan of the buildings was not very different

[1] I subjoin part of the passage at length, "Paululùm remotior ab eodem, est locus dictus Calvariæ, ubi lignum Dominicum trecentesimo octogesimo sexto anno pòst Passionem Christi à beata Helena, Juda præmonstrante, inventum est; ubi etiam ab eadem Regina Ecclesia miræ magnitudinis et operis fundata, postea à perfidis Gentilibus destructa est; (ruinæ cujus adhuc existentes indicant qualenam opus fuerit. Pars autem ligni preciosi in his locis à fidelibus retenta, diligenti veneratione adoratur et exaltatur.) Juxtà crucis inventionem à Meridie est Ecclesia Genetricis Dei quæ *Latina* nuncupatur, eò quòd a Latinis semper sit culta; ubi fertur eadem Virgo plorasse atque scidisse crines, cum vidisset Filium suum unigenitum patibulo affixum" (Gesta Dei per Francos, p. 573.)

from that which they had before the destruction, and it may be supposed that it had been intended to rebuild or repair the other oratories as well as the Round Church, had not the Crusaders conceived and carried out their magnificent plan of uniting the whole under one roof, which I have explained at length in the former part of the Architectural History.

SUPPLEMENTARY NOTES.

NOTE A.

ON THE IMITATIONS OF THE HOLY SEPULCHRE IN THE MIDDLE AGES.

It has been asserted by some writers that the Holy Sepulchre became the primitive type of all other churches of a circular form[1]. If my restoration of the Basilica of Constantine be correct, it is plain that their opinion is destroyed, because I have shewn that no Round Church at all was erected at first about the Holy Sepulchre, but that the Round Church on that spot originated with Modestus, about the year 629. It is true, that in all probability the external form of the Sepulchre was round. However, the Mausoleum of Helena, and that of Constantia at Rome, are sufficient to shew that the circular form of Church was adopted in the time of Constantine, and there is not the slightest reason to suppose that the imitation of the Sepulchre ever entered into the thoughts of the architects of these and similar buildings; for if it had, the fact would have been handed down to us by the ecclesiastical writers of old. One such instance is recorded; for Codinus relates that the Church of the Virgin at Constantinople, called of the *Curator*, apparently from the office of the person who superintended the building, was erected by Verina, the wife of Leo Macela, in the form of the Holy Sepulchre[2]. But as the Church has disappeared, we cannot tell what the plan of it was; but from the expressions employed it must have been in imitation of the Sepulchre itself. In fact, the circular or polygonal form naturally occurs when a building is required for the preservation or enclosure of any single object, such as a tomb or a font; and accordingly baptisteries have been erected in this shape from the period of Constantine downwards. But in the case of the Holy Sepulchre the buildings had the double purpose of enclosing that monument, and of providing a separate house of prayer in its neighbourhood, and hence the more magnificent plan of placing it in the midst of an atrium surrounded by colonnades. In addition to which an opinion seems to have been entertained, that it would be irreverent to cover this monument with a roof. This opinion is constantly alluded to by the mediæval writers; but I am unable to shew that it had an origin so early as Constantine, although

---

[1] See Quarterly Review, March, 1845, p. 356.

[2] εἰς τὸ ὁμοίωμα τοῦ τάφου τοῦ κυρίου. (Codinus, p. 53, ex Originibus C. P. as quoted by Du Cange, Constantinopolis Christiana, p. 86.)

it is not improbable that that was the case. But, indeed, the external decoration of the Cave and its isolation, rendered it quite of sufficient importance to stand alone.

The opinion, that round churches were erected in imitation of the Sepulchre, seems to have originated in modern times from the known practice of the Templars, whose Order was founded nineteen years after the conquest of Jerusalem, and whose round churches therefore were constructed in imitation of the Rotunda erected by the Greek Emperors in the third period of the buildings. But the imitation went no farther than the mere circular plan, which was even sometimes made polygonal, and these Temple-churches had also large eastern chancels, in accordance with that which the Crusaders had added to the Church of the Sepulchre at Jerusalem; but not planned on so magnificent a scale, or with any attempt at exact reproduction. I do not mean, however, to deny that churches were erected in the Middle Ages with a more direct intention of copying the Holy Sepulchre than those of the Templars. One example of such a copy I have given, and another is to be found in the Church of S. Stefano at Bologna.

This Church of S. Stefano was founded, as they say[1], by S. Petronio, in 430, in imitation of the churches of the Holy Sepulchre and of Calvary at Jerusalem; and, united to the Church of S. Peter which (founded in 330) was already there. The early existence of part of this tradition is testified by the bull of Celestine III. (1191—1198), in which he terms the Church of S. Stefano "the Jerusalem of Bologna, which Petronius erected and constructed in imitation of the Sepulchre of our Lord at Jerusalem[2]."

The churches, however, which he built, were destroyed by the Hungarians in 903, and afterwards rebuilt. They also suffered by fire in 1210, and have been subsequently restored and modernised in various ways.

The present church or group of churches which goes by the general name of S. Stefano at Bologna, comprises six, which are packed together in so apparently irregular and unskilful a manner, that Agincourt, in his History of the Decadence of Art, has given a plan of them as an example of the total want of skill and symmetry in the buildings of that age[3]. But if this plan be compared with that of the churches of the Sepulchre in their second period (Plate 1, Fig. 3), we must be convinced that the churches of S. Stefano were really laid out in imitation of the churches at Jerusalem, and therefore that the tradition is not without

[1] Masini, Bologna Perlustrata, p.124.

[2] "Cùm itaque in templo gloriosi protomartyris Stephani, quod dicitur Hierusalem de Bononia, quod servus Dei Petronius, ejusdem civitatis episcopus, instar Sepulchri Domini nostri Jesu Christi in Hierusalem erexit et construxit." (Acta Sanctorum, Oct. T. II. p. 434.)

[3] Agincourt, Plate 28. The work has been lately reprinted in this country, and can easily be referred to.

foundation, although the style of the remaining buildings shews that no part of them can be prior to the destruction of Bologna by the Hungarians in the tenth century.

In the first place, there is a round church supported on twelve piers in a rude Lombard style, surmounted by a clerestory and a dome[4]. In the middle is a sepulchre constructed, as Masini and the guide-books say[5], in imitation of the Holy Sepulchre. However, Gally Knight's view shews in this place a stone pulpit with a peculiar canopy having an altar over it. The church is only half the diameter of the Rotunda at Jerusalem, and the imitation is not to be supposed a very close one. The Round Church has an aisle, bounded, however, not by a concentric, but by a polygonal, wall of eight very irregular sides: this church is called S. Sepolcro. On the north side is a small Romanesque church with a centre and side-aisles, and three apses. This is called S. Pietro e Paolo, and occupies a similar position to the Chapel of the Apparition at Jerusalem; but this did not probably enter into the scheme of imitation; for this is the church said to have been founded before S. Petronius commenced his operations. On the east of S. Sepolcro is a square church, now roofed over, but which was evidently in its original state a cloistered court. It is called "Corte di Pilato," and corresponds to the open court in its Jerusalem prototype. On the south side of it, and partly of the church of S. Sepolcro, there stands an oblong church, the east end of which is raised upon a Romanesque crypt, called the crypt of S. Lorenzo. The body of the church extended much farther westward than the Round Church. This was the church of S. Stefano. It was rebuilt on a new plan, uniting two churches in one, in 1637, and was dedicated to the Crucifixion. Still it is plain that this crypt and its upper church were erected in imitation of the chapels of Adam and of Calvary. There is a sixth church at the east side of the cloister or "Corte di Pilato," which may possibly have been erected in imitation of the Basilica of Constantine; but there is no tradition to the effect that the imitation was carried so far as this. This church was dedicated to the Trinity.

On the whole, I am of opinion that the similarity of plan is quite sufficient to shew that these churches were partly contrived in imitation

---

[4] A view of the interior is given by Gally Knight, Ecc. Arch. of Italy, Plate 20. The piers are not all of the same form; the seven eastern ones are double or compound, and the seven western are simple pillars; this is shewn in Agincourt's Plan. I visited the Church in 1832, but as my attention was wholly directed at that time to the architectural details, I am unable to recall any particulars relating to the arrangement of the plan that would elucidate the present question.

[5] "Un Sepolcro simile à quello di Christo Signor nostro." Masini, p. 124.

of those at Jerusalem. Of course, considering the imperfect state of the art of drawing in those days, it would be absurd to expect anything like a copy or model in such imitations; all that can be looked for is a general resemblance in the plan, carried out according to such architectural details and dimensions as were practised in the period and place where the imitation was made. Doubtless, therefore, the churches in question were erected at Bologna after the destruction of the city by the Hungarians in 903, and the plans made from the accounts and recollections of some pilgrim or other with respect to the churches at Jerusalem as they then existed. And this in consequence of the tradition alluded to in the Bull of Pope Celestine quoted above, that S. Petronius originally erected in the Church of S. Stefano an imitation of the Holy Sepulchre and Golgotha.

The most minute account of this transaction is to be found in the Life of S. Petronius, printed in the *Acta Sanctorum* from a monk's Chronicle, which is continued up to the year 1180 only[1], and may probably therefore be of that age. This writer relates that the Saint built a Monastery in honour of St Stephen..."and that he with much labour completed a work marvellously constructed in imitation of the Lord's Sepulchre, according to the manner which he had seen and carefully measured with a measuring rod when he was at Jerusalem......He erected another edifice with great variety of columns, and with a court round about, with two orders of precious columns with their bases and capitals ornamented with various symbols, and so arranged that upon the lower order of columns another and more ornamental one was placed, and thus extended as far as the place which represented Golgotha or Calvary......And in that place he fixed a wooden cross, which in length and breadth was entirely made in the likeness of the Cross."......And then he proceeds to say, that having measured the distance from Golgotha to Mount Olivet, he made at Bologna an artificial mountain, which to this day is called Mount Olivet, and built on the top of it a Church dedicated to St John, and also he made a reservoir to represent Siloe. If this artificial Olivet be the present Church of S. Giovanni in Monte, the distance is considerably less than the original; for by a plan of Bologna, which is lying before me, I find it to be only 656 feet from one church to the other, whereas the distance of the original points at Jerusalem is 4500 feet. However, the whole tradition appears to me to be a very curious one, and worth investigating, by examining the buildings on the spot with more care than has been hitherto bestowed upon them.

The Sepulchre is more minutely described in a subsequent part of the Chronicle[2], under the year 1141, which states that "there is in the Church of St Stephen a sepulchre which was fabricated by S. Petronius in

---

[1] Acta Sanctorum, Oct. T. II. p. 459.

[2] Ibid. p. 467.

the likeness of the Holy Sepulchre, and that on the right-hand of its entrance is a chest in which the Saint had deposited innumerable relics, and on the left-hand, another chest, which contains the body of S. Petronius himself." This chest was opened in 1141, and the Saint "invented" as the phrase is. This Chronicle furnishes us with some valuable information, which appears to have been overlooked, concerning the dates of part of the existing buildings.

In the account of the above-mentioned "Invention" of relics of S. Petronius and other saints[3], it appears that in the year 1141 the Monks were hunting for a certain chest of relics of S. Isidore and others, which some old men had informed them they had seen under the *Ambo* of the High Altar of the Church of S. Peter, when it was rebuilt[4].

This passage fixes the building of the Church of S. Peter to within sixty or seventy years before this search, and therefore to about the year 1070.

A short time after this, the Abbot and Monks found it necessary to pull down the Church of the Holy Cross, in which the Golgotha was constructed by S. Petronius, in order to rebuild it, and upon digging under the pavement they found other boxes of relics[5]. This narrative furnishes us with the date of the Romanesque Crypt of S. Lorenzo, which occupies the place of the Golgotha of Petronius, and is thus shewn to have been rebuilt about 1145.

In consequence of some miraculous cures of fever in 1307, which were supposed to have been effected by water drawn from a well under the Altar of S. Petronius in this Church, the worship of this Saint grew into great popularity at Bologna, and the great church dedicated to him was in consequence commenced in 1390.

I have thought it worth while to append the above notes to the History of the Sepulchre, because I am not aware that the similarity of plan between the Churches of Bologna and Jerusalem has been noticed before. The fashion of modern writers is to consider the Round Church

---

[3] Acta Sanctorum, Oct. T. II. pp. 466—469.

[4] "...cùm præfati S. Isidori basilica noviter ædificaretur, antiqui, qui tunc aderant, ab una parte eam perspexerunt et prædicto abbati atque monachis ea omnia multotiens retulerunt." It appears from the note, (p. 469. c.) that the chest or coffin of S. Isidore was interred deep in the ground in the Church of S. Peter, which is therefore in the above passage called the basilica of S. Isidore.

[5] "Post aliquod itaque parcissimum temporis cùm à prædictæ ecclesiæ abbate et monachis initum fuisset concilium ut Ecclesia sanctæ Crucis, in qua Golgotha à S. Petronio locus appellatus fuerat, à fundamento murus undique destrueretur, et firmius reficeretur: quem verò ubi statuerunt, fodientes in pavimento ipsius Ecclesiæ, pretiosas repererunt arcas, &c..." p. 468.

at Bologna as the Baptistery of the ancient Cathedral. I have not been able to get sight of the works referred to by Mr. Gally Knight and others on this subject, namely, An anonymous Tract on this Church in 1772, and a History of it by D. Celestine Petracchi.

NOTE B.

ON THE CONFLAGRATION OF THE CHURCH OF THE HOLY SEPULCHRE IN 1808.

THE particulars of the Fire which so greatly damaged the Church of the Holy Sepulchre in 1808 principally interest us, as enabling us to discover what portions of the old structure may remain; and, for the information of future travellers to Jerusalem, I have thought it worth while to add some few notes upon this subject, hoping that by thus directing their attention to it, an examination of the present structure may be made with an especial view to the separation and description of the old portions. I am aware of three principal authorities for the narrative, namely, the account which was published by the Franciscans, the account similarly published by the Greeks, and a private letter which is inserted in the Pilgrimage of De Géramb. They all agree in the main facts, but each party describes its especial effects upon their own portion of the church; and it is only by comparing the different accounts that we can discover the real extent of the damage, or rather the parts that really escaped. It must be confessed, too, that both Greeks and Latins reciprocally are apt to describe with some exultation the ravages of the fire upon the Holy Places of their opponents, and to contrast them with the miraculous manner in which some of their own remained unscathed.

The fire began in the Armenian Church, which is in the triforium of the Rotunda (over 68, Fig. 4), whence it communicated to the great Cupola of the Rotunda, from whence it passed to the Greek choir, thence to their dwelling-places upon Calvary (75, Fig. 5), and to the Chapels of Calvary, where it ruined the beautiful marbles of that sanctuary as well as those of the chapel of the Madonna.

From the aforesaid choir it also passed to the Gallery of the Latins over the north aisle of the Rotunda, reducing to ashes the four apartments and the altar of S. Didacus, and the other apartments, where it consumed the furniture appropriated to the pilgrims, and the carpets, lamps of silver and of other metals, and the *ornaments*. The Turkish dwellings which were over the rooms of the Latins, were also burnt and fell in ruins upon their apartments. After five hours of violent combustion the great cupola fell, and crushed in its fall the little cupola of the Holy Sepulchre, breaking to pieces the columns of porphyry which sustained it, as well as the columns and marbles around the Sepulchre.

De Géramb has given the copy of a letter from an Italian priest, an eye-witness to the fire[1], in which he declares, amongst other things, that the little Convent of the Franciscans, and their Chapel (of the Apparition), as well as the sacristy, had escaped the least injury. The Chapel of the Angel had half its velvet hangings burnt, but its walls and pavements were uninjured. Also the Chapel of the Crucifixion, which belonged to the Latins, was only slightly injured, but the Chapel of the Exaltation very greatly. The Chapel of the Porch was also uninjured.

The Picture of the Resurrection, which closed the Sepulchre, was saved, and even the silk hangings and cords of the lamps. But the Copts' Chapel was wholly burnt.

Mr. Turner[2] gives a transcript of the account which was published by the Franciscan guardians of the Church, entitled, *Breve Notizia dell' Incendio accaduto Nel Tempio del SS^mo Sepolchro di N.S.G.C. il giorno* 12 *Ottobre*, 1808. This history, however, the object of which was to solicit subscriptions for the repair of the fabric, confines its statements to the damage done, without particularising the parts that escaped, excepting only the interior of the Sepulchre. I have quoted some incidental information from it in the course of the preceding pages, and beg to refer to the interesting work of Mr. Turner for the remainder.

Lastly, I have been favoured with a translation from the Russian letter, which was circulated by Callinicus, Patriarch of Constantinople, in order to obtain assistance, and which contains the Greek version of the affair, from which, as it has never been printed, I will give an extract. "On the 30th day of September, 1808[3], on Wednesday, at 8 o'clock in the evening, suddenly and unexpectedly an extensive conflagration took place within the temple of the holy life-giving Sepulchre, and consumed the whole of that wonderful, royal, and holy building, as well as the lofty cupola[4], which was covered with lead, and the small Chapel which was built over the Holy Sepulchre itself: the upper galleries of the Catechumens[5], which went round it, under the large cupola, as well on our side as on that of the Franks and Armenians, are entirely destroyed; for the beautiful marble pillars, on which these galleries were supported, were calcined and burnt. Both treasuries also (the great and the small), and all the cells, the holy ikons (or pictures of saints), the Cross erected on holy Golgotha, the holy Table and Altar of Sacrifice, and the seats of the

---

[1] Pélérinage a Jerusalem, &c. T. I. p. 125.

[2] Journal of a Tour in the Levant, Vol. II. p. 597.

[3] The Greeks still use the old style.

[4] Namely, that which covers the Rotunda.

[5] Commonly called the Triforium-gallery in England.

Patriarchs in the heavenly place, were consumed. When the marble columns on which the arches rested were reduced to ashes, the arches themselves also which were above the Altar[1] were destroyed. The Ikonostasis of the Cathedral, and all the side Altars, together with all the images, and the two thrones of the Patriarch and Bishop, which were in the centre of the Cathedral, became the prey of the flames. Owing to the excessive heat, the lamps and the chandeliers with branches, and the rest of the utensils of the church, were melted like wax. In like manner, the whole of the splendid vestry, the gifts of so many pious monarchs, which were kept within the Temple, disappeared. The holy gates also were burnt, and the cupola, which was above the Cathedral, rent in twain[2].

"The only parts that were uninjured were the subterranean Chapel of the Discovery of the Cross[3], the aisle which surrounds the Church, [4]the holy Chapel of the Sepulchre and its door[5]. All the rest, as we have already stated, was burnt and disappeared."

The narrative then goes on to detail the steps that were taken by the Greek church to obtain authority from the Porte for restoring the building. The architect employed was by name Commenes, a native of Mitylene, and he sailed from Constantinople in the beginning of May, 1809, to commence the work. Difficulties and disputes arose between the Greeks, Latins, and Armenians, concerning their respective shares in the future building, in which each party was endeavouring to overreach and eject the others from the places they had respectively occupied in the ancient arrangement of the churches. Of such quarrels the less said, the better; and I shall merely add, that notwithstanding these, and the delay caused by an insurrection of the Mohammedans, who attempted to stop the works by violence, the new church was completed and consecrated on the 11th September, 1810. It is added, that the cost of the building itself was only equal to one-third part of the sum expended in satisfying the local authorities and conducting the lawsuits. Hence the entire restoration amounted to four millions of roubles.

From these accounts it appears that the roof of the Rotunda was burnt, and its principal wall with the pillars and arches so much injured and weakened by the fire, that it was necessarily rebuilt. How far the vaults of the galleries suffered, or whether the present Rotunda is

---

[1] Namely, in the apse.

[2] The central cupola over the choir.

[3] The Chapel of S. Helena.

[4] This appears to be the most probable meaning of the words in the original, "Glavnia Sviazi," *principales connexus v. colligationes*, but it is an obscure expression, and the translation very doubtful.

[5] This enumeration only includes the parts that the Greeks were interested in, and therefore omits the Chapel of the Apparition, &c. which belongs to the Latins.

a new wall, or merely a casing, must be left for future examination. The outer wall with its apses, the Latin convent and the row of chapels with the Campanile, evidently escaped. Of the Crusaders' church, it appears that the central cupola was split by the fire. However, the piers still remain, as I am informed by Mr. Scoles, and the pointed arches above them are the original ones. The small pillars of the apse and in front of the triforium were evidently calcined by the burning of the wooden fittings of the choir and *Ikonostasis*. But to what extent the vault of this choir suffered, or the vaults that carried the triforium, remains to be inquired. Evidently, the north transept and outer circumference, namely, the north cloister (21) with the prison, the procession-path (24 to 34), and the Chapel of Helena, were uninjured. On the south side, the entrance-front and the porch (53) were unscathed; but there was an unlucky wooden house for the Greeks which stood in the place marked *Greek Kitchen*, [at (75) in Fig. 5,] which in the Latin account of the fire is described as a tower in seven stories. This structure fed the flames, and was the occasion of most serious damage to this quarter of the church; and hence probably the necessity for the changes that have taken place in the arrangements of the chapels of Calvary, which I have described at length in a previous page. Still the stone vaulting of these chapels must remain, and would repay an antiquarian investigation, which I trust will also be extended to the examination of the ancient portals of this church, and to the remains of the Canons' Convent, which I have endeavoured to describe in the seventh Section.

NOTE C.

ON THE AUTHORITIES FOR THE PLANS AND SECTIONS IN PLATES II. AND III.

It may be necessary to give some history of the materials from which I have constructed the Plans and Sections in Plates II. and III.

The only strictly architectural account is to be found in the work of Father Bernardino, "Trattato delle Piante et Immagini de Sacri Edifizi di Terra Sancta, 1620." This contains a detailed plan of the Church of the Holy Sepulchre, together with an elevation, two principal sections, and various other details. There is also an ample verbal description accompanied by written measures. To the entire accuracy of the plan I am enabled to bring the most satisfactory testimony; for the kindness of my excellent friend, J. J. Scoles, Esq., has placed at my disposal an elaborate measured plan of this very church, which he made in the year 1825, and which forms the basis of the engraved plan which accompanies this memoir. It will be found to agree with that of Bernardino in all the numerous irregularities which necessarily belong to a group of buildings erected from time to time upon a rocky and unequal foundation, and partly made up of the ruins of previous buildings. It is true that this plan was taken from the buildings after the fire of 1808; but the changes which were introduced in the subsequent rebuilding affect only the central portion, and although that stands on the old foundations, so that the style of architecture of the principal part of the Church is miserably changed, the plan is only slightly affected, and not at all changed in the outer walls and chapels, as will presently appear.

But although Bernardino is the only author that has given drawings to scale, other travellers have given perspective views and ample descriptions, and from them we are enabled to understand the true value of Bernardino's elevations.

These, I regret to say, are utterly worthless. They represent the Church inside and out as constructed with circular arches, cornices, and in many cases with entablatures of a classical character. It fortunately happens that the entrance-front of the Church, which is at the south end of the transept, is still in existence, and has remained unaltered, except by dilapidation and neglect, from the time of the Crusaders. And the same may be said of the campanile which stands at the side of it, only that the hand of Time has pressed more heavily upon it, and has shorn it of its upper stories, which are represented as complete in Breydenbach's excellent wood-cut, (A.D. 1490), and was yet standing although roofless, in the days of Le Bruyn (A.D. 1725). This façade, however, from its picturesque character, has been made the subject of every traveller's pencil from Breydenbach to the present time, and it is only necessary to compare one of these well-known representations with Bernardino's unhappy elevation in page 23, to understand the process which his sketches must have undergone in preparing them for publication. Every arch in this elevation, both of the church and tower, is in reality a pointed one, the style of the whole being exactly such a pointed Greco-Romanesque as the Crusaders would naturally employ in the latter part of their occupation of the city, when this façade was erected, namely, about the year 1180. But in Bernardino's engraving, the round arches and the projecting cornices, totally unfaithful as a representation of the real building, have evidently been modelled by an Italian artist from the mediæval campaniles and Romanesque structures of Italy; the original drawings being probably of too rough a nature to be sufficiently understood. In the same manner the Chapel of S. Helena, which has pointed arches on rude dwarfed columns, and which still exists, and has been engraved by Roberts and others, is shewn by Bernardino as a light Italian structure upon lofty and well-proportioned pillars with semicircular arches. The only conclusion that I can draw from a most careful comparison of Bernardino's work with every other authority is this,—that his plans, and all his details and explanations, are perfectly honest and faithful, and may be implicitly relied on, so far as the arrangement, disposition, and dimensions of the buildings are concerned; but that he was unable to make drawings of architectural decoration, and that his rude sketches were therefore dressed up for publication after their arrival in Italy[1].

One of the greatest difficulties that I have had to contend with, in the endeavour to discover the original section of the Church, has been the confusion between round and pointed arches in the drawings of travellers. The attention of antiquarians was not until lately, directed to the pointed arch and to the important influence which the forms of arches generally, exercised upon style and history. In their rough sketches, therefore, they never indicated the form exactly, and the artists and engravers, who prepared their drawings for publication, naturally made every arch of the semicircular form familiar to their own eyes, unless a very particular remark to the contrary was to be found in the sketch: for travellers are very seldom able to draw architecture with technical correctness, even if they can draw tolerably any thing else, which is not often the case. Le Bruyn was a professional artist; yet, as we now know, he has repeatedly represented ruins and buildings in his travels with round arches, that still exist to convict him of error. The numerous ambiguities and differences which I have encountered on this head, have almost led me to conclude that if in any given case one authority makes an arch *pointed*, while every other represents it to be *round*, the first is right; because, before the present century, an arch would of course be assumed by an engraver to be round, even if it had been awkwardly drawn as half-pointed or elliptical; and unless it were sketched so *pointedly pointed* that the intention of the artist could not be evaded.

Amongst the various articles that are manufactured by the Monks of Jerusalem for sale to the pilgrims, as memorials of their visit, are to be found models of the Church of the Sepulchre. These are very elaborately constructed, and many of them are in this country, in the hands of different individuals. Two may be seen in the British Museum; one of which belonged to the original collection of Sir Hans Sloane. I find these models very exactly constructed, and giving internal evidence of their truth, in the manner in which the various galleries and arcades of the Church are shewn, and which a practised eye can alone appre-

---

[1] Mr. Fergusson, however, warrants Bernardino's accuracy to the fullest extent. "The most singularly correct work for its age that I have met with anywhere." p. 88. The scales upon Bernardino's plates are wholly inconsistent with the written measures in the text; indeed, the worth of the book is greatly destroyed by the manner in which it is engraved.

ciate. They are not very exactly constructed to scale; but they are ingeniously contrived, so as to be capable of being taken to pieces, to shew the various chapels and recesses. Thus the interior is modelled as carefully as the exterior. They are absurdly inlaid with mother-of-pearl, in various devices, and part of the construction of the building is modified to suit the cabinet-maker's convenience in putting the work together. However, the main point is, that the whole of the eastern part of the Church is represented in these models as having pointed arches, both in the pier-arches, the triforium, and in the great central lantern. The windows are all round-headed. This is so perfectly consistent with what might have been expected, and with the portions that have survived the fire of 1808, that I have not hesitated to adopt their pointed arches in the general section of the Church, although Le Bruyn, who has given us the only view extant of this interior, has made the tower and lateral arches semicircular. But he has done the same by the campanile, or rather given its arches an elliptical form: and yet the lower part of this campanile still stands with pointed arches of the most decided character. As to the great Rotunda, or circular nave, every authority concurs with the models, in making its arches semicircular. It must therefore be clearly understood, that although the plan of the Church, in Plate II., is based upon a very exact survey, and collated with Bernardino's and other authorities, yet that the section (Plate III) has been necessarily filled up in many parts from description alone: especially with respect to the relative altitudes of the pier-arches, triforium, clerestory, &c.; for which I have had to depend upon Bernadino's written measures; in which the sum is not always consistent with the items, and many of which he evidently only estimated by eye. But the most important part of this Section, namely, the relative levels of the Calvary, and of the Church of Helena, to the pavement of the Rotunda, has been supplied from the accurate measurements of Mr Scoles; and with respect to the *general* arrangement of the arches, galleries, and buildings, in this Section, I have no doubt whatever; beyond this degree of accuracy I cannot pretend.

The disposition of the triforium of the eastern apse is involved in much obscurity. Bernardino represents an upper gallery of the full width of the semicircular aisle below, and his description in words, p. 37, seems to imply that arrangement. On the other hand, the models omit this gallery altogether. I am inclined to take the middle course, of supposing that there was a gallery in the thickness of the wall, as I have shewn in the Section. The models also decorate the upper story of the apse with an arcade of nine arches, alternately pierced for windows; and this agrees with the numerous arches shewn in Le Bruyn's sketch, but not at all with Bernardino's.

An accurate research into the existing building by an architectural student, well versed in mediæval structures, would, I am confident, detect sufficient remains of the Church before the fire in 1808, represented in my Sections, to form a much more complete and more exact one; and I trust that my attempt will induce some traveller to set about correcting my mistakes, and resolving the difficulties which I can only pretend to have pointed out; happy if in so doing I shall have succeeded in exciting the interest that always attaches to an object of research once indicated.

DESCRIPTION OF THE PLATES, WITH ADDITIONAL REMARKS.

Plate I.

Fig. 1. Plan of the supposed state of the ground at the time of the Crucifixion, (Sect. IX.) The outlines represent the present streets and the leading points of the plan of the Church. A, the Chapel of S. Helena; B, the high ground to the west of the Holy Sepulchre, which was lowered by Constantine's architects; C, the cliff, in the face of which the entrance of the Sepulchre was formed; D, the catacomb of which the tomb called of Joseph and Nicodemus is the remains; E, Mount Calvary. The hollow between this point and C was the place filled up by Hadrian with earth to conceal the Sepulchre; F, the rock-cistern, called the "Prison;" G I, St Stephen Street; I K, Sepulchre Street; K L, Patriarch Street; L M, the steep descent, which leads to the Entrance Court of the Church; M G, Palmer Street; G I was originally the line of the city wall, and the gate called the Porta Judiciaria was placed at I. The remaining letters of reference shew the points through which the Sections of the ground in Plate III., Fig. 11. are taken. Those Sections should be compared with the present Figure.

Fig. 2. Plan of the Basilica of Constantine. (Sect. X).

Fig. 3. Plan of the churches, as rebuilt by the Emperors of Constantinople, after their destruction by the Caliph Hakem in 1010; according to the description of Sæwulf, in 1103 (Sect. XII), and also in illustration of Arculfus (Sect. XI). A, the Chapel of S. James; B, the Chapel of the Holy Trinity; C, the Chapel of S. John; D, the south-east door of the Round Church; E F G, the three eastern apses, conjecturally supplied; H, the north-east door; I, the Chapel of S. Mary; J K L, the three western apses of the Round Church or Rotunda; M, the Chapel or Oratory of S. Mary over the Unction Stone; N, the Golgothan Church. The outline shews its probable extent in the days of Arculfus; P, the *exedra* mentioned by Arculfus, in which relics were kept; Q, the steps leading down to the Chapel of S. Helena (W) which is called by Arculfus the Basilica of Constantine, and by Sæwulf and William of Tyre, &c., the ruins of the basilica of Constantine; S, the *paradise* or open court; T, the corridor, or cloister-walk which led from the door H to the prison V. There was probably another corridor at R, leading to the Golgothan Church. *a*, the *Compas* or centre of the world; *a b c d*, the outer circumference or outer wall of the triple church, if Arculfus's description be literally correct; but, on account of the great rise of the ground at the west of the church, it is probable that this outer circle extended only through the eastern half *d a b*, where it served as an external *porticus*. The middle wall of Arculfus with its three apses was the same as the present wall L K J in its western half, and its eastern half was probably completed, as the dotted line shews, in the form of a concentric circle, and may have had a fourth apse at F to contain the altar which he mentions. The doors of the circular wall must have been placed opposite the points D and H respectively. *e*, the well of St Helena; *f*, the outer door of the Golgothan church, before which the bodies of the dead were laid while the service was being performed in the apse of the church; *g*, the altar of Abraham; Y, the portal of Constantine's basilica, the remains of which still exist; Z, the position of the cistern, now called the Treasury of Helena.

Plate II.

Fig. 4. General plan of the Church and its adjacent Chapels, as they existed before the fire of 1808. The walls are shaded with four different tints, to indicate, (1) the parts that are cut out of the rock, as far as I have been able to ascertain them; (2) the buildings that existed before the Crusaders' kingdom was established; (3) the Crusaders' buildings; (4) the subsequent buildings and appendages. The side-aisles and lower parts of the Church itself are separated from the central higher parts by a very light tint.

1, The Cave of the Holy Sepulchre; 2, the Angel's Chapel; 3, the platform which leads to it, which is raised three steps above the pavement of the Rotunda; 4, the arch which connects the Rotunda with the choir of the Crusaders, now the Greek Church; 5, the southern apse; 6, the tomb of Joseph of Arimathæa and Nicodemus; 7, the western apse, into which its present door opens; 8, the northern apse: this has a door which leads to the Latin or Franciscan convent, also to 9, the Greek Font, and 10, the well of Helena; 11, the convent-kitchen; 12, the refectory; 13, passages and staircases to the dormitories which are above; 14, the Chapel of the Virgin Mary of the Apparition with its three altars and the seats of the choir: a round stone in the middle marks the place where Christ appeared to the

Virgin; 15, a space at present enclosed as a sacristy for the Latins; 16, the steps leading up to the door of the chapel; 17, this was originally enclosed to form a recess for an altar of S. Mary Magdalene, but is now the door of the sacristy; 18, the arch which leads to the corridor (21) in the place of the north-west door of the Rotunda, corresponding to 67 on the south; 19, a stone in the pavement to mark the place where Mary Magdalene stood when our Lord appeared to her as a gardener; 20, a similar stone in the place where he stood; 21, the corridor which leads to the prison (23) this was part of the original church before the Crusaders began their additions; 22, an altar near which is a stone with holes in it, called the "bonds of Christ;" 23, an apartment hewn in the rock, probably for a cistern, known as the "Prison of Christ." I do not know whether the roof be of rock, or an artificial vault. 24, A door which originally led to the dormitory of the Canons, at the east end of the Church, but which now merely conducts to a small apartment. Part of this is marked in Bernardino's Plan as having been for many years the residence of an anchoret. 25, Chapel of S. Longinus; 26, this opening appears to have been originally designed for a window, it now leads to a little apartment; 27, Chapel of the Division of the Vestments; 28, door leading to the descending stair of the Chapel of S Helena. This stair of thirty steps of marble or stone, is formed in an artificial cleft of the rock, and the rocky sides of the passage still remain uncovered. 29, The Altar of the Good Thief; 30, the Altar of S. Helena; 31, the marble chair in which she sat while the search for the Cross was proceeding; 32, the stairs by which to descend to the Chapel of the Invention of the Cross; 33, an altar fixed on the spot where the invention took place; 34, the Chapel of Mocking; 35, door and staircase leading to the Greek apartments, (See Fig. 5); 37, the patriarchal chair; 38, the High Altar; 36, 39, the side altars. The Greek Iconostasis, or High Screen with paintings and three doors, is placed where the word Presbytery is written, having the steps to the west of it; 40, the seat of the Patriarch of Jerusalem; 41, the seat of the other Patriarchs; 42, the north choir-stalls and screen; 43, the *Compas* or centre of the world; 44, the south choir-stalls and screen; 45, the stairs which led to the chapels of Calvary or mezzanine floor, (described below under Fig. 5;) 46, the arch of the south transept, which opens to the south side aisle of the choir; 47, the Chapel of Adam or of Godfrey; 48, the tomb of Godfrey de Bouillon, first king of Jerusalem; 49, the tomb of his successor, Baldwin I. The double-dotted line shews the screen which formed the boundary of the western part of the Chapel of Adam. 50, The stone of Unction; 51, part of the side-aisle which lies beneath the Chapel of the Crucifixion; 52, a vaulted room, now used as a vestry, and similarly under the Chapel. The floor of the Chapel above is absurdly said by the Latins to be the spot upon which our Saviour was nailed to the Cross. 53, An apartment under the porch of the chapels of Calvary, used as a chapel of S. Mary of Egypt; 54, the stairs leading up to the porch; 55, the south-east door of the Church, now walled up; 56, the south-west door, which is the only entrance that the Mohammedans have left open; 57, door leading to a chapel of S. Michael and All Saints; 58, door to the Armenian Church of S. John; 59, door to the Greek Monastery of Abraham; 60, the remains of a cloister which apparently occupied the north side of the court, or served as a porch to the Monastery of S. Maria Latina; 61, the Chapel of S. James; 62, the Chapel of the Trinity, also called of S. Mary Magdalene and of the Ointment-bearers, and now used as the Greek parish-church; 63, the font; 64, the present entrance; 65, the Chapel of S. John, upon which the campanile is erected; 66, the door into the side-aisle of the Rotunda, now walled up; 67, the arch which was originally the south-west door of the Rotunda before the Crusaders made additions to the Church; 68, a round stone which marks the place where the "acquaintance stood afar off beholding" the Crucifixion. At this point the staircase commences which leads to the principal Armenian church; this occupies part of the triforium overhead. 69, The Chapel of Constantine attached to the Greek Monastery.

Fig. 5. Plan of the chapels of Calvary upon the mezzanine floor, which is in this part of the Church interposed between the ground-floor and the triforium. The exact relative position of this floor to the main building, Fig. 4, is shewn by the chapel of the Mocking 34, the staircase, 45, and the external staircase to the porch, 54; which three points are marked with the same figures of reference in the two plans.

In Fig. 5, 70 is the porch, now blocked up; 71, the first chapel called the Chapel of the Crucifixion; 72, 73, the Chapel of the Exaltation of the Cross. The three holes to the east of the altar mark the position of the three crosses, and the circle behind the apse of the Chapel of Adam in Fig. 4 shews the position of the central hole corresponding to that behind the altar, 72. 74, The chapels of Abraham and of Melchisedech, of the exact plan of which I have no information. I only know by description that they occupy this corner of the building. 75, The kitchen of the Greek apartments, which has other rooms over it.

Previously to the fire of 1808, the mezzanine floor was reached by means of the staircase, 45, which is shewn in the general plan, Fig. 4, and the plan of Calvary, Fig. 5. This floor was also in the Crusaders' time reached by the external stair and porch, 54, 70, so that there was a way up and a way down for the processions of pilgrims. There was also a projecting gallery marked *a b* in Fig 5, which gave access from the Chapel of the Exaltation, 72, to the Greek apartments, 75, by means of two small doors, as shewn in the plan. Since the fire of 1808, however, these arrangements have been wholly changed, and the present plan is indicated by dotted lines in Fig. 5, for the information of travellers who may now visit this spot.

The ancient stair, 45, is destroyed as well as the gallery, *a b*, and in its place a floor on the level of the chapels is carried over this part of the side-aisle reaching from *c d* at the east to *e f* at the west. This floor has a door, *m*, to the Greek dwelling, and a stair on the south which leads down to the north choir-door. The floor of the chapels which formerly extended only to *k* and *l*, is now also carried westward into the south transept by a projecting gallery or screen, *f g h*, which stands partly upon the same place as the old screen of the Chapel of Adam, (marked by double-dotted lines in the general plan at 48, 49). This new gallery has a staircase at *h* rising from a door in the transept at its southern corner, under the triforium-gallery, and close to the blocked-up door, 55. The new gallery has also another staircase at *g* which opens below upon a door in the north end of the screen at *f g*, so that thus a double access is provided, one stair up and another down.

Fig. 6. Conjectural Plan of the Holy Sepulchre as originally fitted up by Constantine.

Fig. 7. Plan of the Holy Sepulchre from the Crusaders' Conquest to the Fire of 1808, copied from Bernardino, (with the exception of the tints that divide the rock from the marble).

Fig. 8. Plan of the present Holy Sepulchre, (from a drawing by Mr. J. J. Scoles).

These three plans are all drawn to the same scale and have the same letters of reference. The rock is shaded with a rough dark tint, and the stone or marble additions with a uniform and lighter tint. A, the loculus or actual sepulchre; B the space in front of it, in which persons may stand; C, the door, the sides of which appear still to exhibit an uncovered rocky surface; D, the Angel Chapel: the square in the midst professes to be, or to represent, the stone which originally closed the mouth of the cave; EE stone seats; FF candelabra introduced into the modern structure; G the platform; H the Chapel of the Copts. This, which previously to the fire of 1808 was a rough wooden construction that may be seen in the drawings of Breydenbach and others, is now permanently constructed of stone or marble.

Plate III.

Fig. 9. A section of the church from East to West. The authorities for which I have explained in Note C. The lines of section are necessarily taken so as to lie behind each other, as no continuous line would pass through the different stairs of the Chapels of the Invention of the Cross, of Helena, and the principal church. The section of the Chapel of the Invention is taken from S westward through the stairs that lead down to it; that of the Chapel of Helena, through its centre and through its stairs; and finally, the section of the principal church is taken through its centre and through the Holy Sepulchre from the eastern apse (27) to the western apse (7.)

Fig. 10 is a section through part of the rock of Calvary and its chapels along the line *x y* (Fig. 4), which will explain the relative positions of the upper and lower chapels and their relation to the rock in which the apse of the Chapel of Adam is formed.

In these sections the rock is distinguished by a rough dark tint, and the masonry by a lighter and smooth tint.

Fig. 11 is a set of east and west sections of the original state of the ground placed upon the same level, the positions of which are shewn upon the plan, Fig. 1. But these sections are drawn upon the same scale as that of the church in Figs. 9 and 10. T V, a section passing through the foothole of the Cross upon Calvary, and therefore corresponding to the section in Fig 10. W, X, a section passing through the Sepulchre, and corresponding to Fig. 9. Y Z, a section passing along Sepulchre Street, and representing it as a uniform slope, from which it probably differs but little.

With reference to the whole of the above figures, I must beg to remark, that many details are necessarily put in from description alone, and that those which represent the original state of the ground, must be considered as illustrating my own views, although based upon pretty correct data. But I surrender them to the criticism of future observers, and shall be most grateful for corrections, or for additional information.

Plate IV.

Plans and sections of the Tombs of the Judges, for which I am indebted to the kindness of Mr. J. J. Scoles. They are described at length in Section IV. In the last page of this section, line 17, for A read H.

Plates V. and VI.

Plans, sections, and details, of the Tomb of Absalom, from the same excellent authority, described in Section V. In this Section I have, however, inadvertently described the plan as lying with the door of entrance to the west, and must beg my readers to make the following corrections:

In the second page of section V, line 3 from the bottom, for *South* read *East*. In line 2 for *North* read *South;* and in line 1, for *East* read *North*. In the third page, in line 10 from the top, for *Northern* read *Western*.

The mouldings and details in Plate 6 are marked each with a letter, and the same letters will be found in Fig. 16, shewing the position of each detail in the monument. The rock is distinguished by a rough dark shade, and the masonry by a light uniform tint, as before. The stones of the masonry carefully marked in from the original. The accumulation of rubbish is also shewn, and it is to be hoped that future travellers will endeavour to supply the measures and details of the base of this curious monument. Cassas has restored it from pure fancy, without noting its encumbered condition.

THE END.

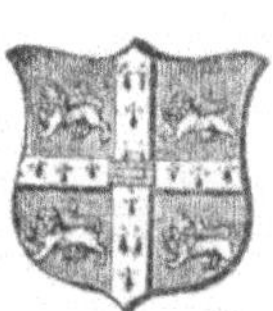

Cambridge:
Printed at the University Press.

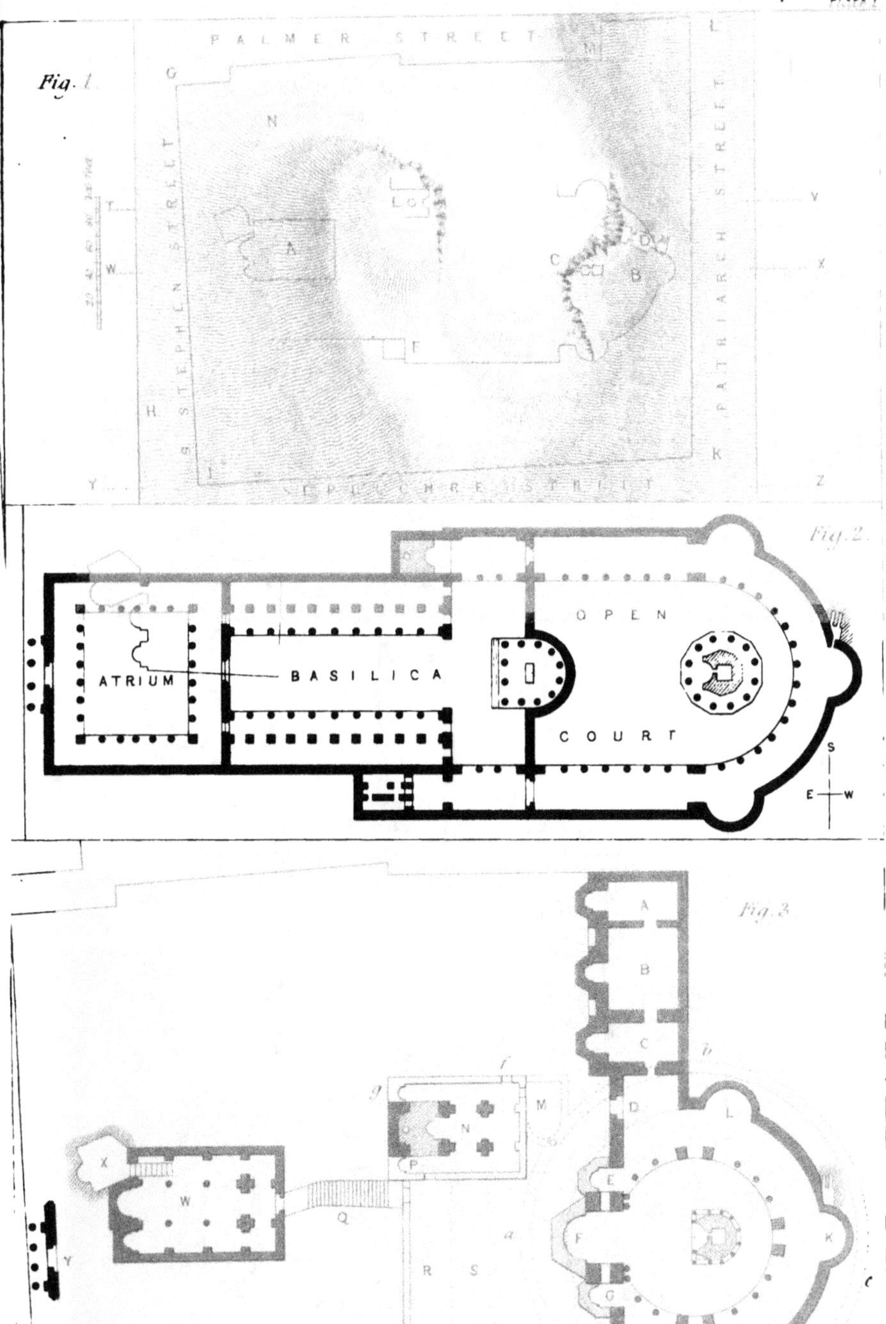

PLANS OF THE CHURCH OF THE HOLY SEPULCHRE.

PLAN OF THE CHURCH

OF

THE HOLY SEPULCHRE.

The Holy ✠ Sepulchre.

1. Entrance to the Church.
2. The Stone of Unction.
3. Where our Saviour was nailed to the Cross.
4. Mount Calvary *+*
5. Chapel of the Sacrifice of Isaac.
6. Chapel of the Altar of Melchisedec.
7. Stairs up to Mount Calvary.
8. Stairs down to the Chapel of St. Helena.
9. Stairs down to the Chapel of the Invention of the Cross.
10. Place where the three Crosses were discovered.
11. Chapel of the Division of the Garments.
12. Prison of our Lord.
13. Greek Choir, in it ⊙, the centre of the world; on each side are the Stalls for the Monks.

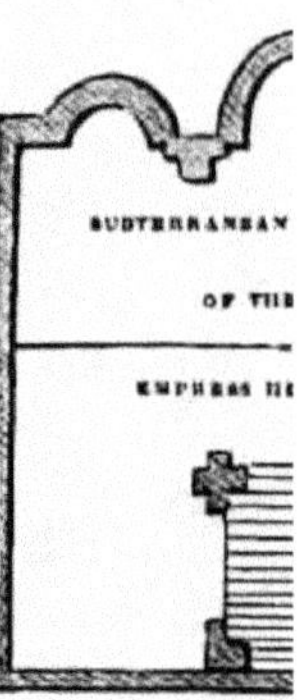

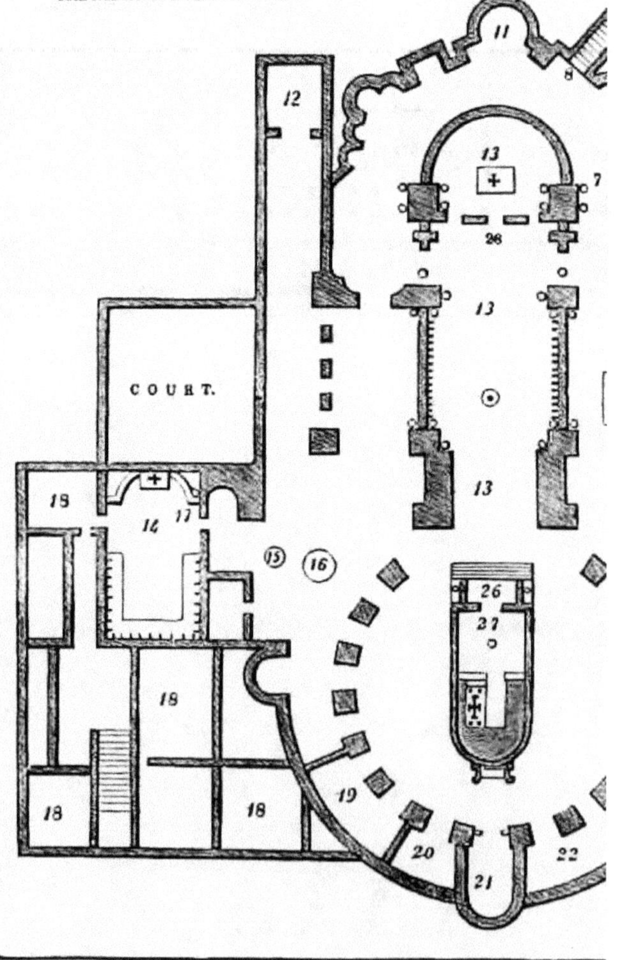

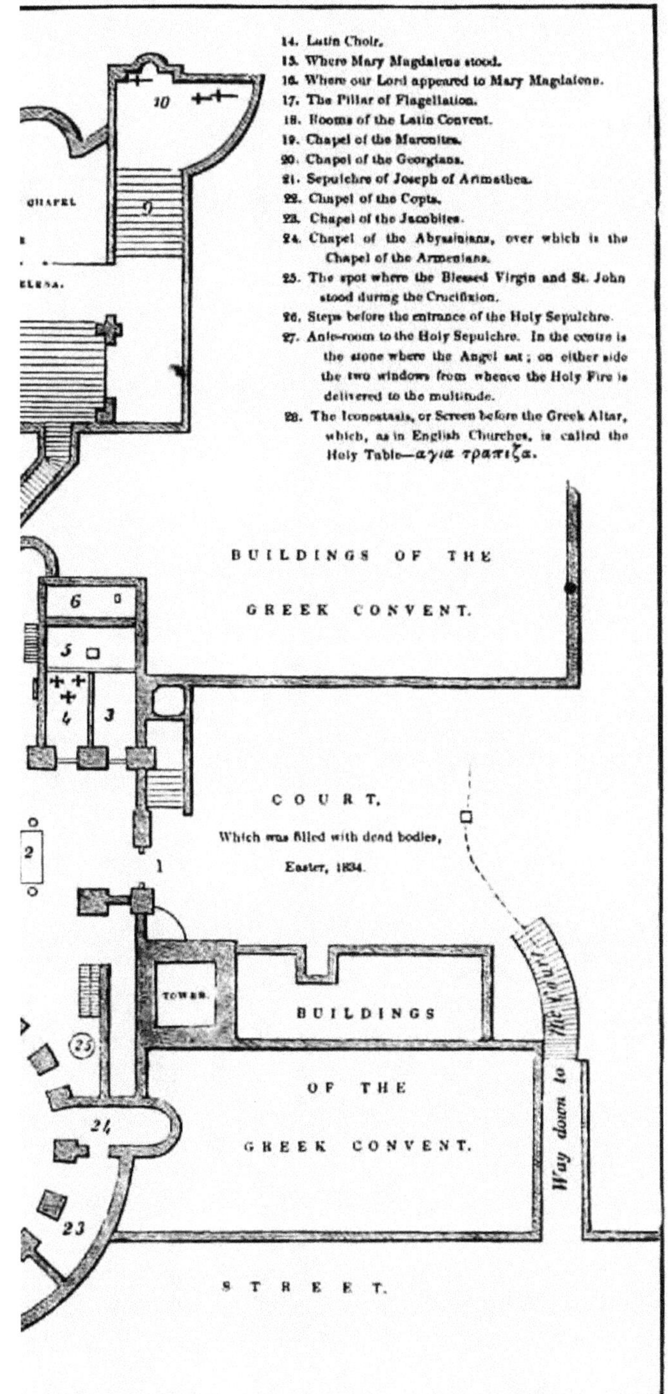
14. Latin Choir.
15. Where Mary Magdalene stood.
16. Where our Lord appeared to Mary Magdalene.
17. The Pillar of Flagellation.
18. Rooms of the Latin Convent.
19. Chapel of the Maronites.
20. Chapel of the Georgians.
21. Sepulchre of Joseph of Arimathea.
22. Chapel of the Copts.
23. Chapel of the Jacobites.
24. Chapel of the Abyssinians, over which is the Chapel of the Armenians.
25. The spot where the Blessed Virgin and St. John stood during the Crucifixion.
26. Steps before the entrance of the Holy Sepulchre.
27. Ante-room to the Holy Sepulchre. In the centre is the stone where the Angel sat; on either side the two windows from whence the Holy Fire is delivered to the multitude.
28. The Iconostasis, or Screen before the Greek Altar, which, as in English Churches, is called the Holy Table—αγια τραπιζα.
CHAPEL
ELENA.
BUILDINGS OF THE
GREEK CONVENT.
COURT,
Which was filled with dead bodies,
Easter, 1834.
TOWER.
BUILDINGS
OF THE
GREEK CONVENT.
Way down to the Court
STREET.

www.ingramcontent.com/pod-product-compliance
Lightning Source LLC
Chambersburg PA
CBHW051514170526
45165CB00002B/463
* 9 7 8 1 4 8 1 0 8 7 9 8 8 *